Handbook of Financial Public Relations

The Institute of Public Relations defines public relations practice as 'the planned and sustained effort to establish and maintain goodwill and mutual understanding between an organization and its publics'.

Handbook of Financial Public Relations

Edited by
Pat Bowman

Published on behalf of
the CAM Foundation

Heinemann Professional Publishing

Heinemann Professional Publishing Ltd
Halley Court, Jordan Hill, Oxford OX2 8EJ

OXFORD   LONDON   MELBOURNE   AUCKLAND   SINGAPORE
IBADAN   NAIROBI   GABORONE   KINGSTON

First published 1989
© Pat Bowman 1989

British Library Cataloguing in Publication Data
Handbook of financial public relations.
1. Public relations.
I. Bowman, Pat   II. CAM Foundation
659.2

ISBN 0 434 90182 2

Typeset by Hewer Text Composition Services, Edinburgh
Printed in Great Britain by Redwood Burn Limited, Trowbridge, Wiltshire

Contents

Foreword

More than a decade has passed since the last definitive handbook on financial public relations appeared, and a great deal has happened since then.

First, the United Kingdom business scene has been transformed from the dark days of the late 1970s, when a large proportion of British industry faced decline, to a new spirit of dynamism and expansion.

Second, the role of financial public relations itself has been not so much transformed as revolutionized. Ten years ago, our activities were viewed by most senior businessmen as no more than peripheral to marketing and advertising, and the primary skill of our practitioners as simply the 'art of communication'.

When the Institute of Public Relations' City and Financial Group was formed, it saw its principal aim being 'to increase the understanding of the role and value of public relations as an integral function of corporate management'.

Looking back over the past ten years, we are, I believe, justified in congratulating ourselves on our achievements. Today our role has been elevated to become much more substantial. Something like three out of every five major British companies now include financial public relations in their corporate strategy and the public relations adviser is more frequently to be found alongside other vital boardroom advisers, such as the merchant banker, broker and lawyer.

The extent to which City institutions are also beginning to appreciate the value of public relations is reflected by the Bank of England and others, where career development now often entails a tour of duty in the press and public relations department.

Quite simply, the reason for this startling rise in the status of financial public relations is that the traumas of the last decade have forcefully brought home the importance of good communication. No company today, of whatever size, can afford to leave its public image to chance.

This increasing demand for our services is reflected not only by the dozen or so public relations firms now quoted on the London Stock Market and Unlisted Securities Market, but by the growth of the public relations market itself. Five years ago it was estimated to be worth some £30m. Today it is valued at well over £100m and growing at some 25 to 30 per cent compound each year.

Our only problem is the classic one of success. There is a crying need for more qualified, talented recruits with a wide range of disparate skills, to meet the ever-expanding demand for good professional advice and service, both in-house and from consultancies.

This handbook is intended not only to help educate those newcomers but to provide management with an appreciation of public relations as a corporate management function, and also to alert potential recruits – executives from the City, law, market research, banking and accountancy, as well as the media – to the outstanding career opportunities which financial public relations has to offer.

In spite of the huge advances made in the perception and practice of the function over the past decade, I suspect we are only just beginning to realize our potential.

Susan Shaar
Chairman 1987–88
City and Financial Group
Institute of Public Relations

Contributors

Richard Bing, BSc, FIPR, has been dealing with investor relations throughout most of his career. He joined TSB Group in 1984 as director of corporate communications to become responsible for all the group's communication activities and to direct a share offer aimed at attracting more than a million shareholders. The flotation was immensely successful: five million people applied for shares, oversubscribing the issue seven times. Previously he was head of public affairs for Rank Xerox, handling investor relations and government affairs, and providing consultancy services to group companies world-wide. Before that he held a number of senior posts in industry and consultancy, dealing with corporate and financial public relations. He is currently director of corporate relations for Southern Electricity, and chairman of the Institute of Public Relations City and Financial Group.

Pat Bowman, FIPR, MAIE, entered public relations after thirteen years as a journalist, becoming public relations officer of the Industrial Society in 1957. After two years there, two as press relations officer of the Bowater Corporation and eleven years as press and public relations officer of British Aluminium, he was appointed head of public relations at Lloyds Bank. After thirteen years there he retired early in 1985 and has since been an independent consultant. He has been chairman of the Press and Public Relations Branch of the National Union of Journalists, a member of the board of examiners and of the professional practices committee of the IPR, and a founding committee member of the IPR City and Financial Group. He was joint editor (with Nigel Ellis) of the *Handbook of Public Relations* (Harrap, 1963) and joint author (with Nigel Ellis) of the *Manual of Public Relations* (Heinemann, 1969, revised 1977 and 1982). He is also author of *The Sponsor's Guide* (Association for Business Sponsorship of the Arts, 1987).

John Cole, MIPR, is a public relations director of Charles Barker City, and specializes in publicly quoted companies and flotations. He joined

Charles Barker in 1971 and has spent more than twenty years in public relations, previously being with the consultancies Preslanders and Voice & Vision. He was a journalist at Heathrow Airport and freelanced in Manchester and Salford. Among others, he has handled the flotation of National Home Loans, the debut of the Templeton fund management group and the arrival of Capital Radio, one of the most successful new issue investments of 1987. His other clients include Boots, Redland and the Clerical Medical Investment Group.

Roger Hayes, FIPR, DipCAM, is chairman of Hayes Macleod, an investor and corporate communication consultancy. Previously he was director of corporate communications for Thorn EMI and before that was with PA, the business and technology consulting group, with responsibility for launching the firm's corporate identity and its new world-wide management magazine, *Issues*. While a vice-president of Burson Marsteller and a director of its UK company, he specialized in corporate communication for multi-national corporations in Europe, the United States and Asia. He began his career as an advertising trainee at Young and Rubicam and a marketing executive at Bodine Electrical in Chicago, before moving to Reuters as a correspondent in Paris. In addition to a BSc (Econ) from London University, he holds an MA (International Political Economy) from the University of Southern California. He lectures and writes on communication subjects. He is secretary-general of the International Public Relations Association and a former chairman of the IPR City and Financial Group.

Charles Hodson is a journalist with the Channel 4 *Business Programme* and was formerly a senior investor relations consultant with Carter Valin Pollen.

John Hollis, who has an honours degree in classics from Trinity College, Oxford, worked in industry from 1953 to 1959. From then until 1976 he was in administration at the Stock Exchange, successively as head of the central settlements department and head of public relations. From 1976 to 1985 he was in Kuwait as adviser on the establishment of a Kuwait Stock Exchange and with a private Kuwaiti investment company. He then joined Dewe Rogerson, becoming a director in 1986.

Peter F. Hutton graduated from Cambridge with a degree in social and political sciences in 1974. He is now a director of Market & Opinion Research International (MORI), where he specializes in corporate image, shareholder, employee, social and political research. He is a frequent writer and speaker on research-related subjects and author of *Survey Research for Managers* (Macmillan, 1988).

Alan Macdonald, MIPR, is head of group corporate communications at Midland Group, which he joined in 1979 as senior public relations officer for Midland Bank International. He was previously a director of Galitzine and Partners, the European co-ordinating office of the International Public Relations Group, and also worked in parliamentary and government affairs consultancy and for J. Walter Thompson. He joined Citibank as a graduate trainee, becoming advertising co-ordinator for the UK and Ireland. He has an MA in law from University College, Oxford, and is a member of the Royal Institute of International Affairs and the Confederation of British Industry broadcasting group.

Angus Maitland is deputy chairman of The VPI Group and chairman of Carter Valin Pollen. He is responsible for the group's world-wide investor relations consultancy resources.

Betty Powell is chief press officer at the Securities and Investments Board. Her background is in the government information services, including the Departments of Health and Social Security and Trade and Industry and the Central Office of Information.

Michael Regester, MIPR, first gained experience of crisis management when, as manager of public affairs for Gulf Oil Corporation, he had to deal with the communication aspects of one of the worst disasters in the history of the oil industry at Gulf's Bantry Bay terminal in southern Ireland. Now a director of Charles Barker Traverse-Healy, he has spent the past eight years advising companies in numerous industries on how to anticipate and deal with corporate crises. He is the author of *Crisis Management* (Hutchinson Business, 1987) and lectures on the subject throughout the world.

Neil Ryder is chairman of the Investor Relations Society and head of marketing and corporate communications for BET. He is also a member of the US National Investor Relations Institute and of the Bank of England's working party on a code of conduct for financial communication for UK quoted companies. He lectures frequently on investor relations to industry and the financial community.

Peter Smith, FIPR, is chief executive of City and Corporate Counsel, which specializes in corporate communication and investor relations counselling to senior management. From 1970 to 1987 he was responsible successively for the corporate relations function in three British companies: Booker McConnell, Powell Duffryn (where he handled the public relations aspects of its defence against a bid from Hanson) and Reed International. He was president of the Institute of Public Relations in 1984 and is immediate past chairman of the Investor Relations Society.

John Smythe, MIPR, is managing director of Smythe Dorward Lambert, a corporate communication consultancy specializing in co-ordinating reputation management and internal attitudinal change. Previously, he spent four years with Wolff Olins, first establishing its successful corporate communication arm, Wolff Olins/Smythe, and then becoming a group executive committee member. He has also held senior public affairs posts with American companies Marathon Oil, The Bechtel Group and Dr Armand Hammer's Occidental Petroleum. He was chairman of the IPR City and Financial Group from 1984 to 1986, and has recently co-founded Mind Link, a specialist interest group of the IPR, focusing on the behavioural and psychological issues of communication.

Colin Trusler is managing director of Shandwick Consultants and a director of Shandwick UK. He entered public relations as the first graduate trainee to be sponsored by the IPR. After six years in consultancy, including spells in New York and Los Angeles, he joined Lloyds Bank as public relations adviser in 1969. He founded the bank's marketing department in 1972 and in 1980 was made head of marketing with responsibility in the UK for strategic marketing activities, including research and planning, product development and pricing, and all marketing communication. With the formation of a corporate communications division in 1983, he was made chief manager and added employee communication to his remit. He joined Shandwick Consultants as a director in 1986.

David Vevers, MIPR, was appointed to the new position of group public affairs manager for the Prudential Corporation in 1985. He had previously been director of communications for J. Rothschild Holdings and before that head of public relations for the Charterhouse Group.

Colin Williams is chief press relations manager of the National Westminster Bank. Originally a journalist in north-east England, Fleet Street and Kenya (where he taught journalism), he moved into public relations consultancy and then to the City Communications Centre, where he became executive director and also executive director of the British Invisible Exports Council. He is an associate and a committee member of the IPR City and Financial Group.

Introduction

Over the past twenty years the business of public relations has expanded greatly and its nature has changed. It has become more scientific, more broadly based, and considerably better understood and used by industrial and commercial management. Over the same period the once isolated world of finance has opened up from the closed community of bankers and brokers, chairmen and directors, accountants and company secretaries to become part of the everyday working environment of the average non-financial executive in large and small concerns alike.

The media have long recognized that finance means more than share prices and that industrial coverage is not solely about labour relations: in other words, that business is news. More recently, public shareholding has grown enormously, speeded by government policy, and the development of electronic communication has led to instant world-wide transactions and information transmission.

The traditional square mile of the City of London is more than ever a power centre for international finance, but new institutions and new techniques, new products and new services abound. Old influences have waned as different regulatory systems have come in. From mergers of multi-national conglomerates to employee share ownership there is movement and innovation everywhere. Providing personal financial advice has become a minor industry in itself. The marketplace has changed out of all recognition and is vastly more competitive than it was a mere five years ago.

No market that lacks communication can operate effectively, for without it there is ignorance and misunderstanding. Thus, financial specialization in public relations has grown up to serve a need and nourish a massive social change.

Corporate public relations executives whose multifarious skills once did not need to encompass any financial experience or techniques have had to realize that no organization exists except in a financial context, and that therefore they have to understand the world of money. Public relations consultancies, specialist or general, have increasingly found that their corporate clients expect financial policy and communication advice as a normal part of the service. Even the old-established City consultancies have had to develop advanced capabilities far ahead of the simple requirements of yesteryear. Many have brought in experts from financial institutions to add their knowledge and judgement to the communication talents of existing professional staff.

The 200 members of the City and Financial Group of the Institute of Public Relations represent a substantial segment of the professional capacity in this sphere of the communication business. Ten of them, all experts in their fields, and five other specialists have contributed chapters to this book, the concept and structure of which the Group committee has approved. All the authors write as individuals and the views they express do not necessarily represent those of their organizations.

No book can hope to be totally comprehensive or remain up to date for long in today's fast-changing world, but here is an attempt to gather together in one volume the elements of financial public relations as they are now. The wider subject of public relations as a whole and other specialized aspects of it are dealt with in other books sponsored by the CAM Foundation.

The book provides guidance for the practising public relations executive who needs to enlarge his or her knowledge of a major facet of the business. It will also serve to prompt the memory of the experienced operator faced with a particular problem. The serious student of public relations will find this book helps to complete the appreciation of the total communication industry which is necessary to achieve examination success. The rising business manager and the management college pupil who wish to learn what public relations can mean to the financial life of their organizations should find it valuable too.

It is a volume intended to illuminate a large, complex and often highly specialized subject and by doing so contribute to the effective communication of financial matters to all audiences.

Pat Bowman

1

Media relations

Colin Williams

'The share price moved on the strength of recent press reports.' That is a familiar and obvious example of the power of the media to influence a company's standing in the financial community. It also demonstrates the importance of media relations within a planned financial public relations strategy which seeks to enhance the perception of an organization's performance and prospects gained by target audiences from analysts to shareholders. Press reports can, and do, shape that perception. So clearly a prime requirement for the effective financial communicator is to know the media market and how to work constructively with it.

The daunting fact, however, is that the financial world is now covered by ever more publications – many of them highly specialized – in addition to receiving increased space in the national press and more air time on radio and television. Concurrent with the resulting growth in media demand for financial news and comment is the changed financial environment in the 1980s. Today's suppliers of financial services are more numerous than ever before, the business is increasingly complex (as is its regulatory framework) and the competition for media exposure has heightened in every sector. In addition, the greater sophistication – and wealth – of the audience cannot be ignored when addressing the public relations task. It needs planning and it needs commitment from the highest executive level if success is to be achieved.

Whatever the changes in the public relations environment, the basic rules of financial press relations have not changed.

Every press call received deserves, and should have, a reply. Even if you draw a blank when looking for the relevant information or the appropriate expert requested, always tell the journalist. Ignoring the question will not make it go away and failing to respond undermines your personal credibility as well as that of the client or the company.

Equally important for your reputation is giving a response within the stated deadline. Knowing the media market includes having a record of individual press and programme deadlines. These can change, so it is worth making a regular check with journalist contacts.

Never guess an answer and never lie. Public relations executives and journalists have a mutual vested interest in accuracy, so check your facts if you are unsure before supplying the media. Giving out untrue information is not ethical, worthwhile or necessary; the alternative is to decline to answer.

Avoiding in-house jargon is particularly relevant in handling financial information. Jargon can lead to confusion and misunderstanding, thus defeating the point of communication. It is far better to turn a complex financial term into plain English whenever possible and gain the benefits of clarity and effective communication.

From the journalists' point of view the information supply on any financial story needs to be accurate, fast and, preferably, direct from the most senior source possible. The public relations executive's task is to meet that requirement within the variations of content and timing that apply to different media outlets.

For specialist writers it is important to ensure that information on company and market trends is provided with supporting detail and access to key spokesmen. Individual briefings complement the specialists' awareness of company strategy and progress, which can be reflected in influential commentaries in the press.

Establish a clear idea of the specific requirements of the writers who specialize in the financial markets, investment, company reports and allied topics relevant to your company's or client's business. Make sure the information you supply meets those needs and arrange regular contact to help them maintain the informed quality of their reports.

As well as working within a different time frame, financial magazines tend to adopt a more analytical approach often one which requires in-depth interview opportunities with company experts. The frequency of contact may be less than that needed by daily paper journalists, but magazines can have a longer 'shelf life' of influence among target audiences.

The national and international news agencies form an important link within the financial news network, where deadlines are instant and the information requirement runs around the clock. Responding to these demands is integral to the financial communication business in view of the agencies' ability to get an important news development around the world-wide media market in a matter of minutes. Their particular requirements are hard facts, short and sharp, with more detailed explanations following.

With the increase in financial coverage on radio and television, requests for spokesmen are frequent, and it is imperative to know the broadcasting capability of nominated company or client representatives. The importance of training should not be underestimated. Good broadcasters are relatively rare in the business world, and time spent selecting, training and assessing spokesmen is never wasted. The ability to provide a good performer who is comfortable with the microphone or camera is an asset which can materially enhance a company's image, as well as help relations with the broadcasting media. As executives change their jobs, regular checks on the pool of trained spokesmen are desirable.

The British regional media carry a substantial amount of commercial coverage, much of it created by London-based City editors. There is naturally a strong interest in news with a local flavour and, wherever possible, local spokesmen are to be preferred. Do not underestimate the influence of the local press and the part it plays in the local business community, many members of which will be your company's or client's customers.

With the development of the global market, the foreign media have an increasing public relations importance and a strong journalistic representation in London. Many of these journalists are financial specialists, but for others finance and business are only part of their brief, so that briefings, etc, need to be adjusted to meet their requirements.

The public relations executive will also have to work with freelance journalists, who, when operating on an uncommissioned basis, seek to develop a story with the objective of selling it to the most appropriate outlet – or outlets. Try to establish from the initial contact that the intended target market is the right one for your company or client.

Similarly, the proliferation of books on finance and the financial world, whose authors are often financial journalists, is a further source of demand for information and interviews. This is one where the inevitably long lead times to publication need to be borne in mind.

Since digging out and supplying the right information at the right time to today's range of financial journalists absorbs most of the working hours in the media relations business, time wastage must be kept under control. Always ensure that you obtain from the start a clear picture of the precise information being sought, how it fits into the proposed story or programme and the level of understanding of the enquiring journalist. It can be less than helpful, indeed counter-productive, to arrange for a technical expert to talk to a non-specialist writer who is simply seeking broad brush comment.

You can also save a lot of time and subsequent heart-searching by determining before you reply exactly what to say and, particularly on issues with commercial or competitive sensitivities, what not to say. Once you have given out information, you cannot call it back. This is not a recommendation for saying nothing; quite the reverse.

While control is advisable in supplying information, you cannot expect accurate assessments and comments on your client or company in the media unless you supply the necessary information. The alternative could be misleading speculation, which may not only be damaging but also take considerably more time and effort to unravel.

Positive financial media relations do not just happen. They have to be earned by working constructively with journalists whether the news is good or bad. Of course the law and company sensitivities do not always make this an easy task, but coping effectively with these limitations will determine the public relations executive's credibility and value as the link between company and media.

Next to accuracy and timing, the form in which financial information is supplied can have a vital bearing on the response produced in the media. The range and volume of financial information needed today make careful explanation imperative if media communication is to be effective.

That thought has to be reflected in the content of press releases, which are at the core of the information supply business. The standard journalistic maxim of 'get the news point in the first paragraph' holds good for financial press releases, along with the need to answer the basics of who, what, where, why, when and how in the rest of the story. Translate all jargon including executive titles, as the internal significance is generally lost on the external audience.

Using releases with a time embargo needs particular care when financial topics are concerned. For listed companies, the Stock Exchange has to be the first recipient of any price-sensitive information, a rule to be strictly observed, so the embargoed release has limited application.

Delivery of press releases is, incidentally, the area which has seen the greatest change, with electronic transmission systems having become more the rule than the exception. Speedy circulation of a press release to the main media outlets via the office facsimile equipment or through one of the growing number of computer-based systems offered by support service companies is a fact of life in the communication business.

Individual interviews or group briefings in support of specific press releases are welcomed by financial journalists, particularly when an important or complex issue is the subject. Such meetings enable a company's thinking on an issue to be fully explained and understood. Remember, though, that the content of the briefing you arrange must justify the journalists' journey. The briefing should be timed to coincide with the issue of the release and be led by the key spokesman, who should also be available for any follow-up press calls immediately after the issue of the release. It is helpful too to have a short summary of the additional points available for handing out at the end of the briefing.

Facility visits, although perhaps less frequently used in financial public relations than in manufacturing industry, can provide another means of communication. Always ensure that the subject is worthwhile in visual terms, has a reasonable mix of 'walk and talk', includes a practical demonstration and that adequate time is allowed for interviews. The mutual objective is a story with some point to it for the ultimate reading, listening or viewing audience. Once again, it is helpful to provide a brief summary of the location, operations, purpose and key spokesmen for the visit.

The formal press conference is a communication vehicle to be used with care to avoid 'devaluing the currency'. For preference, this set-piece event is reserved for only the most important financial news, such as profit announcements, major funding developments and innovative corporate moves such as acquisitions.

Preparatory work should include checking the acoustics of the venue, arranging for a record of the conference by audio tape or stenographer, providing copies of the key opening statements, arranging for telephones to be available for journalists and giving advance notice of the conference schedule to all those attending. Advance discussion of likely questions and their answers, and a rehearsal with the principal spokesmen will be time well spent in helping to identify difficult areas and to brush up conference performance.

Major financial announcements also highlight the increasing overlap of media and investor relations. Journalists and market analysts are in particularly close contact at such times, so it is valuable in public relations terms to have a co-ordinated communication strategy to meet the information requirements of both groups.

An analysts' conference run on the same lines, but separate from and held preferably in advance of the press conference, can help to produce highly effective results. Do not mix the two groups together: their needs can differ and so should their treatment.

The big news event is not the only occasion when that overlap is significant. The frequent circulation of press releases to market and company analysts throughout the year gives an added dimension to the corporate communication business which cannot be ignored. It is advisable to have relevant spokesmen ready to cope with this two-pronged demand.

The background or guidance interview is a familiar feature of financial media relations designed to help journalists obtain a full understanding of market or corporate developments which they can then distil and use without attribution. Price-sensitive information which could affect the market value of shares cannot be handled in this way. Such information has to be precisely worded, kept secure and only made available *after* the relevant details have been lodged with the stock-market authority.

Appropriate security requires observing strict rules on confidentiality when preparing press releases, etc., and limiting the size of the 'need to know' circle.

Confidentiality, especially in relation to customer affairs, is always a key consideration in the media relations of any financial institution. It can be restrictive, e.g. when handling a difficult complaint situation, but it is important to handle this issue with care.

The use of on or off the record comments can cause problems. Always start every discussion with a journalist on the assumption that all comments are on the record. If it becomes necessary in explaining an issue to offer information off the record, then this should be stated and clearly accepted *before* the information is supplied. Some journalists may decline to receive information that is not on the record, so you do not give it.

The press office team is at the sharp end of the corporate/media relationship, with the dual role of information source and the link between company or client and journalists. If it is to perform those roles effectively, the press office must be trusted by both sides – and professionalism is the way to win that trust.

Internally, access to the most senior executive decision-makers and to corporate information, both good and bad, is necessary for carrying out the communication function properly.

It can be useful to have a mix of disciplines to handle the range of enquiries received. Staffing the press office with a blend of trained journalists and in-house technical specialists who have a flair for communication is an approach many financial institutions have adopted, with successful results.

Monitoring the work flow is a routine but necessary task. The most common method is to have details of every press call recorded on a standard enquiry sheet with the action taken noted. Analysis of these records on, say, a monthly basis can help to identify changing trends of journalistic interest and any gaps in contact activity.

A prompt and efficient system for internal clearance of press releases and comment should be high on your action list when organizing a financial press office. Getting the system right at the outset can not only save time later on, but also ensures that the vital requirement of accuracy is safeguarded.

The press office will need another system in order to be kept fully informed about what is happening throughout the corporate structure. A pattern of regular meetings with key executives and department heads is advisable rather than hoping that busy operational staff will remember and find time to warn the press office about newsworthy developments.

It is valuable too to establish a list of personnel who have the authority, ability and willingness to speak direct to the media on their specialities. Updating the list constantly is necessary as roles and responsibilities change.

However good a press office team may be, journalists will always prefer to get their information straight from the market expert or the executive responsible for a particular operation. The job of the press office is to make that happen whenever possible.

Compared to any internal communication system, maintaining relations with media contacts is likely to follow a rather more erratic course and to be largely demand-driven. Do not rely solely on this. If journalists are to build a comprehensive understanding of a company's strategic strengths, then they must have the opportunity to gain an appreciation of the corporate decision-makers. The press office can contribute by arranging a series of informal discussion sessions between top executives and influential commentators. This building process takes time and patience, but it is worthwhile in helping to develop informed assessments in the media, which can, in turn, affect the perceptions held by a wide audience.

Media relations are central to financial public relations. Correctly handled, with expertise and adequate executive commitment, they are capable of influencing the views and reactions of key corporate audiences. So time and well-directed effort must be spent in building constructive relationships with the growing and constantly shifting body of financial journalists.

Increasingly obvious is the need to see media relations within a co-ordinated corporate communication strategy that links to investor relations and so on. This perhaps is the most challenging task that lies ahead of the financial communicator.

2

Investor relations

Professionals and institutions

Peter Smith

The dramatic increase in recent years in both the United Kingdom and
the United States of the unsolicited bid has led companies increasingly
to question their relations with their shareholders. In Germany and
Japan takeovers are generally unacceptable, but they have become
an Anglo-American phenomenon because of the nature of the capital
markets in both countries. Whereas those markets are dominated by
the banks in Germany and Japan, they tend to be dominated by the
securities industries in the UK and the US.

In contrast to common attitudes in Europe, the UK and the US adopt
the position that company boards are almost exclusively responsible to
shareholders. But in practice, particularly in Britain, this relationship has
been weakened by the great size of many companies and the institutional
ownership of the bulk of their shares. Despite the encouragement in
recent years of wider share ownership, spurred on by the privatization
of telecommunications, gas, airlines and the rest, it is unlikely that the
situation in which the majority of the shares of a company are frequently
held by large professional investment groups is going to change.

The growth in information technology has hastened the globalization
of financial markets, has broken down barriers of time and place and made
world-wide instantaneous transmission of information and instructions
commonplace. This represents a risk of greater volatility in market prices
as more major players make their money by taking positions quickly
before the market moves to their disadvantage. In addition, the variety
of choice, the opportunity for hedging and diversification and the ease
of mobilization and transfer of capital have led to a significant widening
of the market for equity. While there are plainly commercial advantages
in this, it also highlights the importance of the development of effective
communication between companies and the investment community.

Although skills, techniques, drive and imaginative management are essential to any healthy company, money is its life-blood. Ultimately its future depends upon the value of its shares, and that value largely depends upon those (comparatively) few people whose judgement decides where money is invested. That judgement will depend upon how much they know about a company's achievements, resources, results and proposed development – in short, on the amount and nature of the information that reaches them.

The central purpose of investor relations is therefore to communicate to the market up-to-date information relevant to the valuation of a company's shares by existing and potential investors, their advisers and those who influence them.

Investor relations is not, and should not be, aimed at pushing up a company's share price. Any such approach would immediately result in suspicion that an acquisition was planned or feared, or a rights issue was under consideration. Properly practised, however, investor relations can help ensure that the price of a company's stock is not adversely affected by false perceptions in the market. While good investor relations is no substitute for good financial performance, it can play a big role in increasing awareness of the future potential of a company.

There are a number of distinguishing characteristics about the financial audience which have important implications for the practice of investor relations. Leaving aside the private investor (dealt with in the second part of this chapter), the audience for most companies is numerically small, thus calling for specialized rather than mass communication techniques. It is a sophisticated audience, so good communication demands intelligent research and efficient planning. Despite its sophistication, it is by no means homogeneous in its information requirements, and therefore a mix of techniques and messages is called for.

The financial audience breaks down into a number of sectors, the main ones being:

1 *Self-investing institutions* – mainly pension funds, insurance companies, investment trusts, and unit trusts. This group of investors is currently responsible for some two-thirds of all investment in the United Kingdom.
2 *Fund management groups* – mainly merchant banks and investment management companies, where the key function is to manage funds on a discretionary basis on behalf of other institutions and private clients.
3 *Stockbroking firms* – subdivided into two main groups with very different functions: equity salesmen and research analysts.
4 *Merchant banks* – in this case the corporate finance rather than the fund management activity. They are key players in finance-raising, mergers and acquisitions.

5   *Employee shareholders* – a growing sector.
6   *Private investors.*
7   *Financial media* – the UK is well served by an articulate and influential financial press, which, although it varies in the quality of its analysis, plays a major role in the market.

Addressing these widely different groups presents companies with a major communication task. In part it is of course compulsory, deriving from the various Companies Acts, the Stock Exchange Listing Agreement, the Takeover Code and, more recently, the Financial Services Act. All of these are required learning and understanding for the investor relations practitioner, as too are the regulations on insider trading, which prescribe what information is and is not price-sensitive (liable to affect the market value of shares), and therefore subject to disclosure to all shareholders when released into the public domain.

The approach of a company in communicating with the small group of large professional investors is of critical importance to the image that is created of the organization and its prospects. More and more this is likely to be done directly, and such contacts are increasingly being viewed as the most valuable – to both parties – of all the various channels of communication.

For the company the information and message can be targeted at the people who really need to know and who are in a position to influence the size of the holding. These are the people who, in the medium and long term, will be held accountable for their investment performance and who, therefore, need and deserve the best possible information. For the institution, direct contact not only gives the fund manager or analyst an opportunity to hear the company's views undistorted but also enables him to ask specific questions of senior management, which contributes a most important means of making a judgement on the quality of management of the company and the coherence and clarity of its plans for the future.

This is not to undervalue, however, the immense importance of creating and sustaining an informed group of sell-side analysts. Since Big Bang, the occupation of the sell-side analyst is almost entirely related to meeting the needs of the major investors, whose trading volume is essential to the well-being of brokerage and market-making activities. For fast reaction to passing events, the sell-side analyst's contribution is indispensable in estimating the effect on the company's performance in terms that the company cannot do for itself in public.

The opportunity that the security analyst gives is to provide an immediate channel of communication to the major shareholders for interpretation and comment on developments as they happen. Given the larger number of big shareholders, and the less detached analysis of individual companies that is undertaken by them, the sell-side analyst provides an efficient means of reaching them quickly with informed interpretations.

An important precondition for a company to be able to communicate successfully is to establish for itself a unique position in the marketplace, namely a clear corporate identity. It is this which articulates what the company is, what it stands for, what it does and where it is going. To be a valuable business reality, the corporate identity must not only derive from the company's corporate strategy, but must also contribute to, and be closely linked into, that strategy. In that way it provides the direction and forms the platform for all the messages to be communicated by the company about itself, both internally and externally.

Therefore the preparation of a corporate positioning statement, which defines the unique qualities and goals of the company and which is both positive and dynamic, should be the first step in planning an investor relations programme.

Market research techniques, to plan and to gauge the effectiveness of investor relations activities, should form an important component of the analysis of shareholders' opinions of the policies and progress of a company and should be of major interest to management in furthering relations with those who own the business. Changes in awareness, opinion and attitude can nowadays be measured extremely accurately. The methods used to monitor them can be as elaborate as major nationwide surveys of many segments of investor opinion or as simple as personal interviews with selected analysts, fund managers, and financial journalists.

While many senior managements pride themselves on close relations with the City, there is usually some difference – often significant – between the information gathered from the company's merchant bank, broker and analyst contacts and that derived from a well designed and professionally executed research study. Although personal contact may result in understanding of broad trends in opinion, it is often useful to have it quantified, particularly when the variable to be measured is specific (for example, how shareholders would feel about the divestment of a key subsidiary) or highly subjective (for example, how analysts rate the management). The anonymity and objectivity provided by independent market research can be critical.

Effective investor relations also requires that there is sufficient knowledge about the characteristics of the company's shareholders. The shareholder register should be analysed, firstly to determine who is on it and how it breaks down between institutional and private shareholders; and, secondly, insofar as the institutional sector is concerned, to identify the major institutions not on the register and, with regard to those that are, to find out whether or not their investment is considered by them to be a core investment.

By analysing the UK equity market and the proportion of it held by the key institutional investors in a company, and by identifying investors who share common investment characteristics, it is possible to construct a desired shareholder profile.

Three further items of information should also be incorporated into this detailed analysis:

1   Who exercises the discretionary control over the shareholding where this is held by a nominee.
2   Who in each fund management institution would take the major decision concerning the increase/decrease of its investment in a particular company.
3   How and on what basis the institutions evaluate the company's present and future performance.

Where a company identifies a strong group of private shareholders holding a reasonable proportion of the shares, it is important to identify who they are; their ages, sex and backgrounds; and how or why their shares were acquired. Whether or not the privatization programme of recent years has stemmed the haemorrhage of private equity investment, a loyal group of private investors is not to be discounted, especially when an unwanted takeover bid is received. Information about them can be most useful in determining such loyalty.

While investor relations is concerned primarily with financial results, it is not always about figures. It is important too to convey something of the spirit of the company and its objectives, as these may well enter into the market judgement of its investment prospects. Institutional shareholders particularly like to assess the quality and development of top management and what resources it has at its disposal.

Other factors by which a company is judged and upon which information is required by institutions and brokers alike are: whether the company is operating in growth markets; its profit record in recent years; its price/earnings record; its dividend record; and its marketing/product expertise, particularly its innovation activities, one important element of which is research and development.

Investor relations provides the link between a company and the financial community in Britain and overseas. Whatever is said or done by investor relations personnel is deemed, by those receiving the information, to carry the approval of the company. The board of directors cannot absolve itself from responsibility for investor relations, and in the event of uncertainty authority should be obtained to act on their behalf.

A company should speak with a single voice and convey a clear, unambiguous message. Ideally, responsibility for investor relations should therefore be vested in a single individual. Where a number of people, including the directors, carry this responsibility co-ordination is essential.

A main purpose of investor relations is to help the financial community and investing public to evaluate a company. Its role is to provide comprehensive information for independent assessment and not actively to promote the purchase or sale of a company's shares.

No audience is privileged in investor relations. Employees, shareholders and potential investors have equal status in terms of the listing agreement with the Stock Exchange. Identical information should therefore be available and given simultaneously to all audiences, including employees, investment analysts and the media.

To avoid creating a false market in the shares of a company, it is important not to convey price-sensitive information to an individual or group of individuals, rather than the market as a whole. The emergence of a global market in securities has made this obligation international as well as domestic.

Yet investor relations does not simply consist of making available and disseminating information. Close personal contact with the financial community also provides the company with a clear insight of how it is perceived by investors. At best therefore investor relations encourages a two-way flow of awareness and should never be used as a barrier between the company and its audience.

The media of communication with shareholders are printed, audio-visual and oral. The typical investor relations programme of a major and active (in communication terms) UK company is likely to include a combination of all three.

Printed communication with shareholders may include:

1   *The annual report*, which is the primary medium of communication in investor relations and a secondary medium of communication with the non-shareholder employee, community, distributor and supplier publics. It is the one opportunity each year to tell shareholders and other publics what the company has done, is doing and plans to do. It reflects a company's image and the calibre of its management, and it may attract new investors and affect the share price.
2   *The interim report* and other materials such as notices of annual and regional meetings, fact books containing financial and operational data, other shareholder booklets and promotional material.
3   *Special offers* to shareholders.
4   *Financial advertising* at the time of the preliminary and interim results.

5 *Annual report advertising* to merchandise the most important share-holder communication of the year.
6 *Corporate advertising* to keep the financial community and the private investor informed on a more regular basis than that allowed by the financial calendar.

Audio-visual communication may take the form of:

1 *A corporate video*, featuring the company and its activities, dealing with a specialist subject, or visualizing the company's annual report.
2 *Financial advertising on television*, although its use is restricted by Independent Broadcasting Authority rules.
3 *Closed circuit television broadcasts* of the annual meeting transmitted to regional meetings of shareholders in other parts of the country or world.
4 *Slide/tape presentations* for meetings of institutional shareholders, analysts and the like.

The principal methods of oral communication with shareholders and the financial community include:

1 *Annual shareholder meetings.* Although many companies seek to get them over as quickly as possible, some companies make them an important corporate event, providing an opportunity for the senior management of the company to establish personal contacts with the people who own and supply the finance to operate the business.
2 *Regional shareholder meetings* when these are appropriate.
3 *Site visits* for institutional shareholders and broking analysts.
4 *Personal visits* to major shareholders.
5 *Meetings* with analysts and members of the financial community.
6 *Financial media relations*, mainly with the financial press but also with the relevant business and trade press. The financial press is important in two respects: firstly, it has a crucial role in communicating with the private investor; secondly, it is an important medium for the professional, supporting as it does a variety of information about the activities of companies and their managements, all of which help the professional to maintain a total dossier on the company and often influence him or her in investment decisions.

The financial calendar is the schedule of key dates during the year on which companies announce results and the periods during which companies may discuss them and significant changes in trends with investors, analysts and the media. It is desirable for companies to establish closed seasons at other periods, which often operate for two to three weeks before the year end or the half-year end until the relevant announcement of results is made.

While investor relations should be vested in a single individual, that person should be providing on a day-to-day basis the necessary planning and support to senior management. The investor relations function should not be the voice and face of the company, although it may be the most regular point of contact for analysts and the media.

Acting as the face and voice of the company must be the job of the chairman, chief executive and finance director. In this context the role of the finance director is extremely important. Wherever the investor relations function is placed in a company, and it is best that it should report directly to the chairman and/or chief executive, the contribution of the finance director and his colleagues should be central to the planning and development of the investor relations programme.

Private investors

Richard Bing

We have come to know instant coffee and instant photographs over the years; more recently we have had the instant mass share register. Many people on these new registers were first-time buyers, new recruits to the share-owning democracy.

British Telecom, TSB, British Gas, British Airways, Rolls-Royce, BAA and, to a lesser extent, British Steel all made giant share issues and acquired millions of shareholders overnight. None of these companies previously had any experience of investor relations. They were catapulted into a position of leadership, whether they liked it or not.

For millions of ordinary men and women these much publicized issues, and others, represented their first adventure in share-ownership. What a tragedy it would be for the concept of wider share-ownership if these new shareholders felt that British Telecom did not know how to communicate, that TSB did not know how to look after their money, that British Gas could only talk hot air, or that British Airways could not get an idea off the ground! Not to mention the problems of handling a market downturn or collapse, a recession in a particular industry or a profit shortfall affecting share values or income.

Many people became new shareholders because they were already customers or employees, or both, of the company coming on to the market. Disappoint a shareholder and you may disgruntle a customer; lose a customer and you may lose a shareholder. Furthermore, a bad experience as a shareholder can have still further repercussions if that shareholder is also an employee. If widespread share ownership is to be really meaningful, companies, particularly those with large share registers, and government too, must be alive to the aspirations and requirements of the small shareholder.

To begin with, what at minimum is the shareholder normally going to get from the company of which he is a stakeholder as well as part owner? There is the annual report, which includes a notice of the annual general meeting (to which, of course, he is invited), an interim statement (and sometimes quarterly results as well), and final and interim dividends.

The annual report, the AGM and the interim statement provide the principal opportunities for communication with the shareholder. They are major marketing opportunities. Dividend payments are less of an opportunity, in that the logistics mean that use of these occasions for mailing other material is limited. The risk of mislaying a dividend cheque among a pile of other paper is real, and no shareholder wants to lose his regular return on his investment.

A marketing approach to shareholders can mean the addition of selling or corporate material, and even special offers for shareholders. Discounts on goods or services are an excellent way of earning shareholder goodwill, not to mention incremental business. The example of cheap cross-channel ferry tickets is probably the best publicized shareholder perk.

Perks can take other forms as well. A hotel group has organized gourmet weekend breaks at selected hotels at discounted prices for its shareholders. The proverbial widget company could not do that? Well what about a shareholder visit to the widget factory? Or a flight on an Airbus powered by engines that depend on widgets? Initiatives such as these can be valuable for shareholders and as examples of corporate promotion too, reaching a much wider audience than just those turning up on the day. They give a very clear indication that the company is trying hard, is forward-looking, innovative and good to be with.

Writing, designing, printing and mailing the annual report always seems to be a mammoth exercise. The task of packaging a report for millions of people is even more daunting. An annual report contains a mass of statutory and more often than not indigestible material, much of which is likely to be incomprehensible to the new investor.

As an example, the first TSB Group annual report was designed to be clear and intelligible, and despite a mass of information was constrained within 28 pages. It was made as attractive as possible within the confines of statutory requirement, size, weight and the messages that needed to be conveyed. With it was included a marketing folder describing some of the group's products and services, plus an explanatory letter from the chairman.

As an aside, there is a strong argument for provision to allow the mass mailing of abbreviated accounts – on the principle of the mini-prospectus – but with the full report being available free of charge for anyone who wants it. When shareholders have commented on the suggestion, the concept of a less technical document has been strongly supported. The building societies have that provision included in the Building Societies Act; whether they take advantage of it will be another matter.

The mass flotations, with their special appeal to the small and new shareholder, brought a large number of ordinary men and women in as first-time investors, but the very size of this army of recruits raises some practical problems when it comes to making arrangements for an annual general meeting.

Legally, companies are obliged to provide for all those who want to attend. The smallest shareholder has the same right to come along, to participate and to vote as the largest shareholder. As another aside, and another legislative point, it would be valuable in later years to have the facility to conduct AGMs with shareholders in different locations at the same time. Some companies have provision in their articles of association to allow them to do just that. Apart from the requirement to change the law, which will no doubt eventually be done, at the moment the technology is not totally risk-free, and more experience of running massive meetings would be helpful before taking that step.

The AGM is a marvellous opportunity to acquaint shareholders with the business, and to hear their own views. It is also a first-rate marketing opportunity. In TSB's case, for example, many shareholders are already users of one or more of the group's products or services, but there is wide scope for interesting them in using the others. The marketing ploy used is 'Now you own it – use it!' Even if shareholders do not want to use the services, the AGM gives them the chance to learn more about the activities of their company.

In a financial services group the opportunities for product promotion are immense. Companies with other products or services perhaps have fewer opportunities but, given a marketing-driven or at least communication-driven policy, an interesting and constructive package will emerge. For TSB at its first AGM at the Scottish Exhibition Centre in Glasgow the group as a whole was featured in an exhibition in the central piazza. Around that hub were displays of the individual subsidiaries in the group.

For shareholders who cannot make their way to an AGM, regional meetings are an option. Such meetings must be held after the AGM and do not have any legal standing. They offer the same opportunity as the AGM to both the shareholders and to the company. Evening sessions as well morning or afternoon ones, so that people at work can attend without having to take time off, are important, because although we talk affectionately of Aunt Agatha, she is by no means the typical small shareholder of today. Elderly Aunt Agatha may well be at leisure to attend an afternoon meeting, but the younger, working man or woman could hardly be blamed if they did not see attendance at an AGM as a good reason for being away from their factory or office.

British Telecom has a shareholder register of some 1.3m (compared to 2.3m at the outset). Its first AGM was held at the National Exhibition Centre in Birmingham, which could have coped with 20,000 shareholders; the number actually attending was about 4,500. At later AGMs the numbers were somewhat lower, and TSB and British Gas have had much the same experience. BT also pioneered the use of large regional meetings, although it was not unique in having local gatherings for shareholders.

The logistics of these large meetings are formidable, and require the experience and expertise of professional conference organizers to set them up. The objectives need to be set out clearly. While not every company's requirements would be precisely the same, the objectives set by TSB would be relevant to the underlying concerns of many organizations.

The objectives were the following: to discharge the company's statutory duties; to present, and be seen to present, a clear picture of the company's financial performance and prospects (orientated to the requirements of the average shareholder); to provide an appropriate forum for answering shareholders' questions about the company, its performance, its service to the customer, or their shareholding; to present the strength of the company's management; to promote a favourable image of the company as a commercially orientated, but nevertheless socially responsible, organization; to promote the company's products and services in a manner consistent with the character of the meeting; and, finally, to present the event with a style and image appropriate to the company.

In short, the event has to meet statutory requirements, to do the best possible job of investor relations (and meet the requirements of the communication policies of the company) and also make the most of the opportunity to promote the company's products and services. Obviously a lot of thought and planning has to go into ensuring that these elements are all properly balanced and harmoniously orchestrated.

A big AGM might go like this. Open the doors at 1 pm to give people time to look around, and show an audio-visual presentation at 2.40 pm as a prelude to the formal meeting which begins at 3 pm. The A-V brings the company story up to date and includes some highlights and successes. After the statutory proceedings, a second A-V show aims to close the meeting in a positive way, presses home the message about products, draws attention to the product range and encourages shareholders to visit the exhibition before they leave.

Video is also used during the formal meeting so that speakers and questioners can be seen on a large screen behind the stage. Any shareholder wishing to put a question is asked to do so from a video booth, so that the audience can see the questioner.

All the footage shot at the meeting is available afterwards for editing into a recording of the event. Many companies use video for training and for employee communication, so full use can be made of the set-piece A-V presentations and of the film record of the meeting itself.

Logistically, taking a hall at somewhere like the NEC or the Scottish Exhibition Centre is akin to renting an enormous, empty aircraft hangar. You need it a few days early to have thousands of seats put in plus a stage, a set, lights and cameras. It is not too different from staging a pop concert. (The mechanism might be similar, but the analogy is not one to push too hard at a company chairman!)

The build-up schedule must include time for rehearsals – several even – including one the evening before in front of members of staff, who could include all those actually helping on the day and any of those who work and live locally. Rehearsals are important too for the platform party. Going on stage in front of a few thousand people and coping with the electronic gadgetry to manage the meeting is a far cry from the average AGM with which directors are familiar.

Shareholders may well have a number of questions on their minds, prompted by the AGM proceedings or perhaps by the exhibition, so within the display areas there should be clearly identified shareholder information stands. The immediate aim is to answer shareholders' queries, and to deflect detailed product or service or share register type queries away from the formal AGM. This should be seen as an opportunity for the company to discover more about what information shareholders find useful. That understanding should then be helpful in sharpening the relevance of the facts and figures supplied to shareholders through the whole communication effort during the year, and particularly of what is directed specifically at them through shareholder mailings.

Regional meetings should follow, as far as possible, the format of the AGM, although there will not of course be any formal statutory proceedings, with resolutions, votes, etc. The set-piece A-Vs can be used, and members of the board should be on the platform to speak and to take questions. Directors and managers should be freely available to meet and talk to shareholders on these occasions. Nothing is worse than the platform party quickly disappearing from view as if it were avoiding personal contact. Local business and political leaders can be invited to come along. Local staff can be there to greet the guests and run the exhibition. The company's local activities can be featured in the displays.

AGMs and regional meetings provide significant platforms from which a company can explain itself to its shareholders, and to interest them in their company and in its products and services. A wider audience is reached as well, as it is not only shareholders who will be exposed to the proceedings or reports of them.

The possession of a large shareholder base means that there is a substantial money and management time cost to all these activities. The task of the communication specialist is to ensure that the cost is justified, and that it is balanced against all the opportunities.

The emphasis so far on large share registers and large meetings has been deliberate because doing it on a big scale forces a concentration on objectives, logistics, methods and implementation. In fact, the same approach is valid for any public company with any number of shareholders.

The objectives for an AGM are relevant for the entire spread of a company's relations with its shareholders. They are, after all, stakeholders in the enterprise and they need to be identified with it. Private shareholders are not normally fickle, but their loyalty cannot be stretched indefinitely and in a takeover bid or battle their votes can be crucial.

So how else to reach the shareholder? Primarily through the media, both in editorial coverage and maybe advertising. Informed City editor (or any other editor, come to that) comment is vital in building confidence about a company, and shareholders will benefit from and be influenced by that comment and confidence.

The process is self-reinforcing and the total communication exercise should be planned to ensure that all the key audiences get the right message, at the right time and in the right way. Journalists are influenced by analysts, for example, and a programme which does not deal with or take into account all the audience groups will leave the company and its shareholders at a disadvantage.

Advertising has its place: financial advertising at the time of the final or interim results and maybe corporate advertising as well. The need and balance will be determined by the company's objectives and the perceived strengths and/or weaknesses of the company, which may well have been identified and quantified by research.

Potential shareholders and the City are intimately entwined in the sense that if City opinion – which can be defined as the key financial analysts for the brokers and the institutions and the key financial journalists – is not convinced that a particular new share offer is good, confidence will go down because comment and coverage of the flotation will suggest it is a poor deal. This applies equally to a big share offer as to a small Unlisted Securities Market flotation.

Services to shareholders can also include a telephone enquiry point, and for companies with retail or other public outlets, regularly updated information notices.

The mass marketed flotations have demonstrated the realization that selling the abstract notion of equity investment does not work. People are more likely to buy a part of something they are familiar with and confident about. Hence the broad corporate messages at the beginning of a campaign. These are followed by an 'alert' stage (letting people know a flotation is happening), a 'maintenance' phase to keep the pot boiling, an 'action' phase to get the money ready, and the final prospectus phase.

For these issues the technique has been to get a bandwagon rolling. Generating a lot of enquiries among potential shareholders makes it a news story, therefore the media must write about it. Talking to the analysts who rate the shares adds to this, as does talking to the media. There is the feeling that it will be a popular stock, and that the institutions and others are not going to be able to get as much as they want. The general public perceives that everybody is doing it and therefore it must be a good thing. It is a talking point, and nobody feels a fool by going out and buying stock.

The big campaigns have used every communication device available, including media advertising (TV, press, posters), direct mail, display and, particularly for intermediaries and staff, roadshows with film, video or slides. Slides can range from one-at-a-time to cross-fade to multi-slide, multi-projector spectaculars.

Shareholder relations is but a part of a company's communication activities. From a corporate point of view, everything a company does and says should be consistent throughout. The messages must be consistent and all the audiences, both internal and external, need to get the appropriate messages, appropriately packaged and at the right time.

For the small, and perhaps unsophisticated, investor 'appropriate' needs to be given extra thought. To take just one example, forms should be written and designed for total clarity and understanding. If a potential shareholder cannot easily fathom out an application form, he will start off being alienated and there may then be extra cost and trouble in sorting out errors. The moral is to get it right before it gets to the shareholder.

Shareholders, whether private or institutional, deserve proper, professional attention. Applying the same marketing and communication techniques to dealing with shareholders as to, say, customers undoubtedly pays benefits. What better benefit is there than a loyal and enthusiastic private shareholder base.

3

Annual reports

John Cole

Researchers tell us that the private shareholder spends on average just one minute looking at an annual report. Considering the time and effort put in, it is perhaps one of the few documents that is read more before it is published than afterwards.

The news value of an annual report is usually taken away by the earlier announcement of the preliminary results (in effect, an abridged version of the report if the company's communicators are doing their job). Unless a report breaks new ground, or there is a special interest, journalists writing for the next day will merely check on a few points: whether the accounts have been qualified by the auditors, or if there has been a dramatic increase in the chairman's remuneration (and if there are any cheap share options or lavish golden handshakes), before noting prospects for the current year.

Analysts following the company's market sector will systematically devour it from cover to cover, and institutional shareholders will give it a reasonably thorough read. Close probing will come not from shareholders, but from would-be predators, competitors and pressure groups.

Extravagant or plain, satisfying or a tedious necessity, the report and accounts is the most important document a public company produces. Yet when it is published, it is already out of date – an historical picture of a company's trading and financial position taken on the last day of its financial year.

Findings show that an annual report is a shareholder's main single source of information about a company; also it is recognized that positive investment decisions are influenced as much by familiarity brought about by good communication rather than exclusively by good performance. Pick up several annual reports at random: do they instil confidence by projecting a successful and well ordered company or leave you confused and ill-informed? Do they make you want to read them? Do they stand up to the 'widow in Bournemouth' test? It is easy to lose a shareholder's attention by lazily resorting to technical jargon when plain language can be understood by everyone.

Reports and accounts must be published and sent to shareholders once a year, no longer than six months after a company's year end, and received at least 21 days before the annual general meeting. Many companies start planning theirs soon after the current issue is delivered from the printers.

Whether starting afresh or to keep pace with the latest trends, the first task is to prepare a critique of the previous report by gathering informal comments from analysts, shareholders and colleagues. If a report has been radically changed, or regularly at intervals of, say, three years, it may be advisable to carry out a more structured research study.

Then, for comparison, take in a collection of a dozen or so admired reports from companies, large and small, in similar and other markets. (*The Observer* runs an excellent company reports request service every Sunday.)

Select your team: finance director, chief accountant, writer, designer, investor relations manager and public relations manager or consultant. Compile a glossary of financial terms, or at least ensure that you are all talking the same language – cash flow might be thought to be money which passes through the tills, but on a net basis it will mean profits retained by the company to help finance itself.

Next, agree a budget, produce a timetable, commission photographs and get estimates from three or four printers. One major company surprised itself by saving £20,000 when it put its substantial print run out to tender for the first time in three years. Another cost-saving measure is to use a word processor to make changes to the text until it is in final form. A multitude of author's corrections and weekend working can make an expensive nonsense of the best intentioned printer's quotes.

All good reports have a purposeful identity or theme. Marks & Spencer has called its report 'Sharing in Success'; Burton came up with 'Successfully Managing Change'; Redland's was 'Progress through Partnership' (Figure 3.1); Boots featured its product range of medicines and cosmetics (Figure 3.2). Capital Radio used its cockney sparrow symbol on the cover (Figure 3.3).

Figures 3.1 to 3.3 show three front covers that avoid the platitudinous while making basic points in a visually attractive way.

It has long been common practice for almost every public company to give more information than is necessary to comply with its statutory obligations and the Stock Exchange listing agreement. Without the extra material a report would be lean and dull. Not even a chairman's statement is necessary and companies would be left with not much more than the profit and loss account, balance sheet, source and application of funds, geographic analysis of turnover and trading results, make-up of

Figure 3.1 *Redland tackles the common need to demonstrate international partnership with an imaginative photo-montage; this report won the 1987 award for the best annual report by a large public company sponsored by* The Accountant *and the Stock Exchange*

Figure 3.2 *Boots says a great deal with just five products displayed in a dynamic form, plus a telling hint of internationalism*

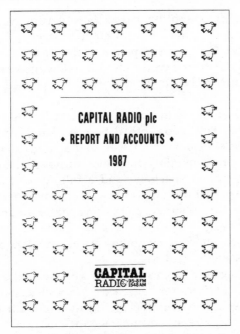

Figure 3.3 *Capital Radio, newly launched on the market, emphasizes its previously under-utilized cockney sparrow symbol*

the board, directors' remuneration and their contractual arrangements, and the notice of the annual general meeting.

Companies also need to produce by law a report of the directors which must give information about major changes in the business and cover results and dividends, principal activities in brief, directors' holdings, acquisitions and disposals, changes in capital structure, fixed assets, policies on employees and disabled persons, research and development, and political and charitable donations.

The chairman's statement should encapsulate the company's year and its achievements (even acknowledging its failures?). In addition, there is often a chief executive's report, sometimes one from the finance director and even divisional reviews. Although too many reviews can be repetitive, they can demonstrate strength and depth of management.

Analysts rely on facts and figures more than opinions and illustrations. In a Charles Barker City survey on what makes an annual report valuable, analysts responded by requesting:

- 'Good presentation of statistics . . . as much breakdown as possible; not just the big numbers, but the small ones that make up the big ones.'
- 'Divisional breakdowns on the basis of turnover and profits.'

- 'A product: profit split by market as well as by company.'
- 'A comprehensive five- or ten-year summary.'
- 'Information on how a company is doing related to its industry.'
- 'A statement on intentions for the following year . . . Sensible long-term predictions by management as opposed to platitudes.'

Earnings per share is the most crucial factor of financial performance, but other key ratios should be considered for inclusion, such as returns on sales, capital employed and shareholders' funds, profit per employee, profit margins and stock turnover. Figures on market shares, a value added statement and a full account of research and development expenditure can also help to give a wider appreciation of a business. A historical summary tracking the profit and loss accounts over five or ten years can be expanded to include balance sheet extracts and capital expenditure. Breakdowns of shareholders by type are also becoming increasingly frequent.

Good habits usually catch on. Three years ago the *Financial Times* praised The BOC Group for being exemplary in displaying full group borrowings, specified by currency, maturity and coupon (rate of interest). Now most progressive companies include these details. A later feature by BOC was a double page year-at-a-glance spread (Figure 3.4) presenting key financial information in chart form. BOC's shareholder information is shown in Figure 3.5.

Some reports have such an array of glossy pictures and dazzling visual devices that they overwhelm or confuse, obscuring the aim of a report to inform. A priority must be to place content and good communication on a higher plane than design. Reg Pauffley of Pauffley & Co, who has designed BOC reports, has admitted: 'Designers must convey the message and not produce a design for its own sake. Sometimes design can actually get in the way of the message'. In seeking to create something new, some designers avoid the obvious. Has there yet been an improvement on the good, old-fashioned pie chart?

To whom should you entrust an annual report for advice on content and creating a design? Some companies continue with good results to use the design departments of printers, but the trend is towards employing public relations consultancies specializing in investor relations or graphic designers experienced in financial work.

In the UK we have had our first pop-up report but we have been spared the more extreme gimmicks from the US. Allied Supermarkets put its report in a brown paper bag; Warner Communications went punk (chairman Steven J. Ross shimmered with purple tints); for seven years spice maker MacCormick has impregnated its report with its tangy flavours; and office furniture maker Herman Miller published a photograph, 1½ inches high, of each of its 3,265 employees. 'We try to go beyond the financials', explained chief financial officer Richard H. Ruch.

There has been a move by some public companies, particularly those privatized concerns which have a large number of shareholders, to issue simplified reports. Although it is debatable whether such initiatives are to save money (the TSB report is said to have cost £1.8m) or to encourage more attentive reading, they are now supported by the government. The Department of Trade and Industry has agreed that listed companies are to be allowed to send their shareholders short summaries. Some believe that most small shareholders are put off by a mass of figures and financial information largely of interest to analysts and more sophisticated investors. Naturally, such companies point out that a copy of the full version would be available on request, but there is a problem in identifying which shareholders should receive which document. In the US the movement is already under way: the irrepressible Herman Miller sent shareholders a poster.

Auditors act on behalf of shareholders as owners of a company, not the directors, and shareholder approval is needed at each annual general meeting to confirm their reappointment. If the annual accounts do not give a 'true and fair' view of the state of affairs and profit or loss, more detailed or additional information must be provided.

If the auditors disagree with information given by the company, they have the right to inform shareholders and are able to make their views known at the annual general meeting. Such a presentation is rare.

The audit team work *in situ* at the company and randomly examine the accounting records to establish their accuracy and test systems. Their role, other than the obvious one of auditing the accounts, can be as broad or narrow as the company wishes. The report of the directors is merely 'reviewed' and is not, strictly speaking, subject to audit. There is no obligation to vet the chairman's statement, but it is rare for an auditor not to check it for accuracy and fairness. A 'true and fair view' clearance will largely apply only to the accounts, that is the profit and loss account, source and application of funds and the balance sheet. Areas within these sections where auditors will be tested, however, are numerous. For example, whether a particular cost is judged extraordinary or exceptional will have an effect on earnings per share (an exceptional item will reduce earnings, an extraordinary amount will not by being taken 'below the line' in the profit and loss account). Asset valuation, off-balance sheet funding and contingent liabilities can also be controversial issues. A more recent debate has centred on putting a value on bands.

The accounts hinge on a company's accounting policies, which define how standard practice has been applied, as they can offer alternative treatments to the same problem. The policies section in a report will

YEAR AT A GLANCE

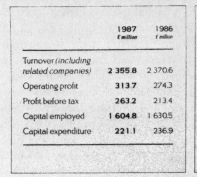

	1987 £ million	1986 £ million
Turnover (including related companies)	2 355.8	2 370.6
Operating profit	313.7	274.3
Profit before tax	263.2	213.4
Capital employed	1 604.8	1 630.5
Capital expenditure	221.1	236.9

	1987	1986
Dividend Dividend per share (including tax credit)	17.5p	15.2p
Employees Number of employees at year end	37 488	37 677

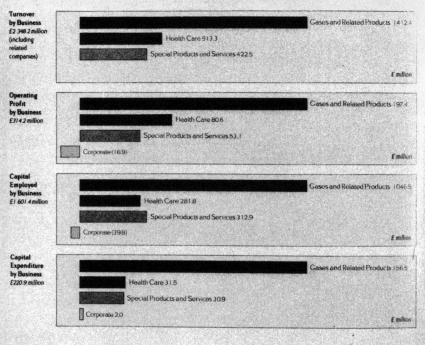

Analysis by Business (continuing businesses)

Turnover by Business £2 348.2 million (including related companies)
- Gases and Related Products 1412.4
- Health Care 513.3
- Special Products and Services 422.5
£ million

Operating Profit by Business £314.2 million
- Gases and Related Products 197.4
- Health Care 80.6
- Special Products and Services 53.1
- Corporate (16.9)
£ million

Capital Employed by Business £1 601.4 million
- Gases and Related Products 1046.5
- Health Care 281.8
- Special Products and Services 312.9
- Corporate (39.8)
£ million

Capital Expenditure by Business £220.9 million
- Gases and Related Products 156.5
- Health Care 31.5
- Special Products and Services 30.9
- Corporate 2.0
£ million

2

Figure 3.4   *To the inexperienced shareholder the weight of detail in many annual reports is overwhelming. Here the BOC Group presents the essentials of its trading year in a deceptively simple form, where intelligent use of block charts takes over from a confusing mass of figures*

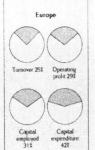
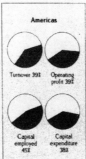
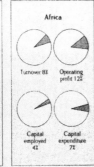

Europe

Turnover 25% Operating profit 29%

Capital employed 31% Capital expenditure 42%

Africa

Turnover 8% Operating profit 12%

Capital employed 4% Capital expenditure 7%

Americas

Turnover 39% Operating profit 39%

Capital employed 45% Capital expenditure 38%

Asia/Pacific

Turnover 28% Operating profit 20%

Capital employed 20% Capital expenditure 13%

Analysis by Region (continuing businesses)

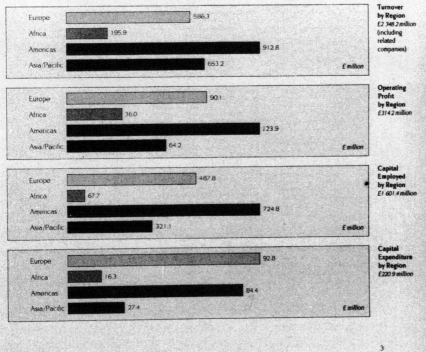

Turnover by Region
£2 348.2 million (including related companies)

Europe	586.3
Africa	195.9
Americas	912.8
Asia/Pacific	653.2

£ million

Operating Profit by Region
£314.2 million

Europe	90.1
Africa	36.0
Americas	123.9
Asia/Pacific	64.2

£ million

Capital Employed by Region
£1 601.4 million

Europe	487.8
Africa	67.7
Americas	724.8
Asia/Pacific	321.1

£ million

Capital Expenditure by Region
£220.9 million

Europe	92.8
Africa	16.3
Americas	84.4
Asia/Pacific	27.4

£ million

3

SHAREHOLDER INFORMATION

Analysis of Ordinary Shareholders at 30th September 1986

Number of accounts	Per cent of total number of accounts	Size of holding 25p shares	Number of 25p shares	Per cent of ordinary capital
15 774	32	1-500	4 123 230	1
12 879	26	501- 1 000	9 740 831	2
18 180	37	1 001- 5 000	36 501 040	8
2 065	4	5 001- 50 000	27 790 139	6
627	1	50 001- 1 000 000	140 284 704	31
79	-	Over 1 000 000	231 088 062	52
49 604	100		449 528 006	100

The Company is not a close company within the meaning of the Income & Corporation Taxes Act 1970 and subsequent legislation. There has been no change in that status since 30th September 1986.

Lloyds Bank Plc maintain the Register of Members and any questions about personal holdings or notification of changes of address should be addressed to Registrar's Department, Goring-by-Sea, Worthing, West Sussex, BN12 6DA.

Financial Calendar

Dividend payments	date paid
Ordinary shares	
Interim announced May	October
final proposed December	April
Preference shares	30th June and 31st December

Announcement of Group results	date announced
Three months' results	February
Half year's results	May
Nine months' results	August
Year's results	December
Report and Accounts	December

Shareholders who wish to receive copies of the interim statements should apply to the Group Manager, Investor Relations, The BOC Group plc, Chertsey Road, Windlesham, Surrey GU20 6HJ, England.

Figure 3.5   *Two basic elements of shareholder information that are often wrongly regarded as of minor importance are in the BOC Group annual report given proper prominence and by clear typographical design made instantly comprehensible*

describe the company's particular method of accounting for such factors as acquisitions, depreciation, stock valuation, foreign exchange, leases and pension funding; any change in policy is also noted.

Most of the elements they cover will have a direct effect on profits. Depreciation, for example, is a charge against profit which recognizes that the assets of a company do not last for ever. If too much depreciation is taken out of the profit, then the accounts will show a lower profit figure. Alternatively, too little will show a higher profit. This may mean that insufficient money is being put to one side to replace the assets. Stock valuation can be a contentious issue: if valued at a figure higher than it can be sold for, that is the equivalent of taking next year's profit into this year's accounts.

The trend for companies to give extra material often means that the pages which extend, amplify or illustrate the accounts actually outweigh them. For example, only 16 pages of the Burton 1987 report, packed as it was with additional information, were audited from a total of 56. In practice, most auditors are consulted on content and how facts, figures and opinions are presented. Auditors too welcome the fashion for lively presentation as long as it does not 'stretch' the truth. But there is some concern that the growing number of sections companies are being encouraged to provide are beyond the reach of the profession. As one senior partner points out: 'Compared with a flotation prospectus where every item has to be cleared and a letter of consent from the accountants delivered to the directors, an annual report is relatively free of restraint. However, a good auditor will support more informed presentation.' Accountants are themselves not beyond self-promotion – Touche Ross signed off its report for Hall Engineering and added its own logo.

Willis Faber neatly solved the problem of how to present both statutory and corporate information in its 1985 report. Shareholders received two documents: the first was the report showing a picture by day of its Trinity Square head office on the front cover and the second, showing Trinity Square by night, was a brochure featuring the group's structure and history and focusing on such of its business sectors as aviation, space, and marine. The two were packed into a two-tone jacket.

For its 1987 report Allied Lyons enrolled the talents of Ivan Fallon, deputy editor of the *Sunday Times*, and photographer Lord Snowdon to tell the story of its Canadian acquisition Hiram Walker in 18 pages.

US foods and household goods producer Sarah Lee, while short on impressive photography, sticks its corporate neck out like few UK companies. Sarah Lee states its 'mission' to be 'a leading consumer marketing company in the US and internationally by manufacturing, marketing and distributing food and consumer packaged goods through retail outlets; products and services for the food service industry and consumer products through distribution channels that are direct to the consumer'. Its financial goals include: a return on equity of at least 20 per cent, real earnings growth of at least 6 per cent per year and keeping the ratio of long-term debt to invested capital below 35 per cent.

In another section on financial performance Sarah Lee faces the acid test of shareholders' expectations by stating that the 'best measure of management's performance is the increase in stockholder value over time relative to alternative investment opportunities'. Then follows a bar chart showing that Sarah Lee's value has easily outstripped US treasury bills and the Standard and Poors 500 stock market index over one, five and ten years; and no less than four senior managers discuss in the report their strategies for future success.

Glynwed's key financial objective is growth in earnings per share, which progressively rose from 11.66p in 1982 to 27.47p in 1986. A bold chart showing this is the first thing you see on opening the 1986 report.

Although less specific, Sunderland brewer Vaux states: 'The aim of the directors is that the company will increase real earnings per share, particularly in the long-term, by developing each business to its potential and at the same time looking for new opportunities and reacting positively to changes in the marketplace.' It goes on to stress its commitment to customers, employees and the community to 'conduct a business with high standards of probity'. One of the few small brewers not to be taken over by its larger brethren, Vaux ends its own mission statement by saying that the best way for the company to achieve its aim is for it to remain a 'strong and independent regional company'.

Burton won acclaim when it produced a stunning report for 1986. The *Financial Times* called it user-friendly and referred to its 'glossy cover, high fashion features, whizzbang photography and up-to-the-minute art direction'. Flick through a copy of Burton and you might be turning the pages of *Vogue* or *Harpers and Queen*, it said. The achievement of Burton and designer Michael Peters was that it compelled shareholders to read it. Although stylish, the 1987 report lacked the impact of the 1986 version, but the mission statement was kept: 'To become Britain's pre-eminent fashion retailer'.

In reviewing its 1987 Annual Report Awards, won by carpets company Crowthers, *Business* magazine asked: 'Has design gone perhaps too far at the expense of lucid prose and crisp financial information?' But the judges agreed that the visual dullness of yesteryear had vanished, while the function of the annual report as a corporate brochure has been generally acknowledged.

Crowthers' large, easy-to-read print and good product photography were liked, but in other reports the judges were critical of over-elaborate or conflicting charts, overdone visual devices, irrelevant cartoons, plain covers ('If they were paperbacks, no-one would buy them'), poor quality printing, inadequate paper – and the suspicion that the heavy hand of the chairman was sometimes at work 'in the desire to be conventional'.

There was criticism of a reliance on too many smiling faces, although some handled people well by showing them in a working context or featuring employees who had made helpful suggestions to a company. Cable and Wireless's prose disappointed the panel, which felt it did not do justice to a dynamic company; Redland's was liked for explaining and commenting upon the figures and for its biographies of directors; Reckitt & Colman was praised for the use of percentages with its financial highlights; and (it was said) readers of Gold Greenlees Trott's report had to wait until page eight to find out that it was an advertising agency.

No other financial publication (except a flotation prospectus) can match the annual report for significance or weight of information. Interim statements are the poor relation and do not even have to be sent to shareholders if companies publish them in at least two national newspapers. Most interim statements are cleanly produced, but most lack imagination; few are illustrated or carry charts or diagrams and rely basically on the profit and loss account, a chairman's statement and declaration of the dividend.

In the US even quarterly reports would put some British full accounts to shame. DIY and builders' products retailer Lowe's is packed with information running to 12 closely printed pages and has a newsy approach. In one story it gives itself a well earned pat on the back by announcing that its 1986 report, selected from 1,000 entries, received the Gold Award from *Financial World* magazine. A feature worth emulating in Lowe's quarterly report is a section on investor information giving details of dividend payment dates, shareholder services, stock exchange listing details – and a telephone number. How many UK companies put that in an annual report? There is also a 'disclosure policy' note which states: 'Lowe's Companies Inc, for more than 25 years, has maintained a policy of complete and free disclosure of all information needed by investors to determine whether they should buy, sell or hold Lowe's stock. The company seeks new and fresh ways of presenting financial and other information about itself to better inform the investor. Your comments are always welcome'.

To recapitulate, if the job falls to you to prepare a company's next annual report, remember a few basic rules: plan carefully, combine informative financial statements with clarity, use compelling visual elements – and do it with style.

Glossary of terms used in the production of an annual report:

Assets: all the things of value which a business owns. They include land, buildings, plant and machinery, vehicles, fixtures and fittings; these are fixed assets. They will also include stocks of goods for sale, cash, money at banks, debts owed by customers; these are current assets.

Auditors: the accountants who verify a company's accounts (the audit) and then certify that they reflect a 'true and fair view' of the business.

Balance sheet: statement of assets and liabilities; a snapshot of a company's financial position on one particular day (the year end).

Capital: money put in to finance a business; capital expenditure is what a business spends on fixed assets; a company's share capital may be its authorized or issued capital; capital employed is total assets, less liabilities.

Cash flow: a company's retained earnings after tax and dividends.

Consolidated accounts: the combined balance sheet and profit and loss accounts of a group of companies. They may also be called group accounts.

Contingent liability: sometimes a business is not sure whether it will have a liability for a particular item or not, as it will only arise at some time in the future if something else happens.

Coupon: nominal rate of interest attached to a fixed interest security.

Creditor: a person or a business who has supplied goods, but who has not yet received money in return.

Current assets: assets which the business uses or consumes or converts into cash.

Current liabilities: debts which a business must pay in the near future – not later than 12 months from the date of the balance sheet.

Debtors: people who owe money to a business for goods or services supplied to them on credit.

Debenture: loans secured on assets of a company; debenture stock may be split into units and traded on the Stock Exchange.

Depreciation: charge made by a company in its profit and loss account to allow for loss in the value of fixed assets.

Dividend: amount which a limited company pays to its shareholders as their share of the profits each year.

Equity: the ordinary share capital of a company, as distinct from its preference or loan capital. Equity shareholders own the company.

Gearing: ratio of debt to equity capital.

Goodwill: an intangible asset, represented by customers who buy from a particular business rather than to go to another. A value is placed on goodwill when a proprietor sells a business or there is a change in ownership.

Liquidity: assets which can quickly and easily be turned into cash.

Loan stock: if a company needs more capital than its authorized capital permits, it may issue loan debenture stock, in return for cash. This stock is sold on the Stock Exchange and holders are entitled to a rate of interest prescribed.

Ordinary shares: shares which ordinary shareholders own. They have a right to receive a share of the profits after the company has met all the other claims.

Preference shares: those which carry rights to a fixed dividend ranking ahead of a dividend paid to ordinary shareholders, but behind claims of loan and debenture holders.

Reserve: amount retained in the company in order to help it to earn future profits.

Share premium account: where a company makes an issue of shares at a price which is higher than their nominal value, the extra amount is called the share premium. It is a capital reserve and the business cannot use it to pay dividends.

Source and application of funds statement: a statement prepared at the same time as the profit and loss account. It shows where the money has come from during the period and how the business has used that money.

Work in progress: covers the value of items which the company has only partly manufactured at the date of the balance sheet.

4

Internal communication

David Vevers

Internal communication, regrettably, is the Cinderella of public relations. Moreover, in too many instances to enumerate, it shows – not against the practice of public relations and internal communication itself – but to the detriment of companies which, at best, have failed to formulate a consistent internal communication strategy and, at worst, have neglected to implement any programme at all. Although attitudes have shown signs of improvement in recent years, particularly among leading concerns, it has to be said that there is still a lamentable lack of corporate appreciation of the vital necessity to communicate fully with employees, on financial and policy issues in particular.

While one hesitates to make these criticisms, nothing is gained by leaving them around to fester. To some they may appear to be sweeping allegations. Unhappily, there is all too sufficient evidence to support the claims. It can be found in surveys carried out in recent years. Market and Opinion Research International, for example, undertook a survey for the *Sunday Times* in 1985 which showed that companies had regressed rather than progressed in their approach to employee communication.

When employees were asked if their company kept them fully or fairly well informed, only 37 per cent responded favourably, compared with 56 per cent who were asked the same question in 1976: a drop of 19 per cent over nine years. In response to another issue – 'the company does not tell us much about what is going on' – the responses showed that 23 per cent agreed with the statement in 1985 compared with 16 per cent nine years previously: an increase of 7 per cent.

While the survey showed employees' attitudes – inevitably a subjective judgement, although not to be ignored on that count alone – it would appear that little comfort can be drawn from the management side. A survey conducted by Vista Communications in 1987 showed that 52 per cent of senior managers thought that communication in their companies was average to poor. Drawing on responses at chief executive or board level from 339 large companies employing in total 2.5m employees, the survey showed that only 48 per cent believed their communication to be good or very good.

Other surveys carry not dissimilar messages. Clearly, they are to be ignored at the peril of companies living in an increasingly competitive world. To quote Linda Moseley, head of the employee relations department of the Confederation of British Industry: 'Good internal communication is not altruism or a luxury. It is good business sense'. A 1986 report prepared by the Warwick University Industrial Relations Research Unit suggested that employers can only blame themselves for the lack of progress in the United Kingdom towards the integrated personnel management techniques exemplified by the Japanese and United States subsidiary companies in Britain, of which internal communication is a vital part.

To switch from the Cinderella metaphor to that of the builder, internal communication is as important to the enduring success of a company as solid foundations are to the longevity of a building. One can design the most prepossessing building in the world – a façade radiating confidence and corporate pride (intrinsically another arm of external public relations, it could be argued) – but if the footings are unsound, eventually the cracks will begin to show.

Similarly with internal communication. An uninformed staff becomes an apathetic staff, and apathy, like rising damp, weakens the edifice upon which relations with the outside world are built. Employees have to be regarded as a company's most valuable asset, a fact recognized by the best employers in the amount of time and money spent on their welfare and training.

Employees should also be a company's best ambassadors. If well informed about the activities and attitudes of the company, they not only feel a strong sense of corporate loyalty but can spread the message to the outside world through daily contacts with family and friends. They can become an enduring advertisement for the corporate image, as vital and effective as any solus site or editorial column inch in the press.

The pace of change experienced in recent years, whether it has been on the more competitive edge of British industry or the revolution in financial services, is bringing about a different attitude to internal communication, although not necessarily at the same speed as the general change itself. Increasingly, however, enlightened companies are taking a more positive attitude. One has only to look at the approach of Woolworth or British Airways, to name but two, to see what can be done to bring employees into company affairs.

Woolworth went through a traumatic time in 1982 when Woolworth Holdings was formed to take over the United Kingdom interests of the American Woolworth Company. Nigel Whittaker, corporate affairs director, recalled:

When we walked in, morale had never been lower. Not unnaturally, there were major concerns among staff at all levels. Did the takeover really disguise an asset-stripping programme? Could the new team effectively turn the ship round? Would the company survive long enough to see long-servers to retirement? The company had produced poor figures for some years. Our high priority was to win staff support and gain commitment to a new strategy.

The new management devised a strategy which started by gauging the various constituents of the 'problem'. Accordingly, it carried out an attitude survey among 20,000 employees. The 85 per cent response produced some clear messages: fear was apparent at all levels, management meant 'I tell; you do', communication was poor throughout the company, bureaucracy was rife.

The managers had been conditioned to be managers of systems, procedures, stock and property. People were there to be directed, manipulated and disciplined. The managers were treated as bureaucrats. Creativity and initiative had neither been expected nor rewarded.

Communication had to be a high priority, although Nigel Whittaker, with hindsight, will counsel that in setting out an internal communication strategy it is imperative not to take on too much at once, because it can lead to expectations demanding excessive time to be fulfilled. He argues most strongly that an effective programme will only work if it has the 100 per cent backing of the chief executive. Without that personal commitment an internal communication strategy loses its impact and impetus through delays.

Whittaker and his colleagues turned the company newspaper into a bustling vehicle of communication. 'We took an early decision that we had to be brave enough to print controversial views and that senior managers had to be prepared to come forward with honest and straightforward answers to criticisms', he says. Moreover, any important news had to be communicated to employees before they read about it in the national press.

Line managers were seen as crucial to the exercise. Not only were they to be put through training programmes, but in the early days 1,500 of them attended a series of conferences – there were eight a week – throughout the country, conducted by senior executives. The conferences were deliberately structured to be 'hair shirt' sessions, the managers being encouraged to ask probing questions.

Woolworth, in carrying out its strategy, was underwriting a fundamental principle. Attitudes to work are important and employees expect a lot of their managers. Today they have higher expectations and aspirations, and are heavily influenced by society around them, especially their schools, universities and the media. There is a growing need for companies to explain the economic facts of life. Although there has been considerable technological advance in methods of internal communication, it is still a fact, revealed by the results of the Vista Communications survey, that most communication in companies is still handled via circulars and notice boards. A growth in team briefings, however, is shown, with 71 per cent of respondents making use of this method. The use of video achieved a 49 per cent response.

In spite of the activity that has taken place in British firms over the past few years, two major difficulties still remain to be overcome. In the first place, many firms still do not know how their communication policies actually work in practice. Secondly, according to evidence, a number of them have little idea if they work at all. Furthermore, they do not know how to find out!

The communication audit is increasingly becoming standard practice among enlightened companies. Just as an audit for the accounts takes a snapshot of the company's financial position at a given time, so the communication audit is a snapshot of the way communication actually functions. It is not influenced by what someone stopped doing six months ago, nor by what somebody intends starting on Monday. It is simply an objective picture of what is happening now compared with what senior executives think, or have been assured, is happening.

The Prudential, for example, carried out communication audits, in 1985 and 1987. The contrasts between the two are revealing, partly as a result of the action the company undertook on the basis of the first audit.

What did that first audit reveal? Firstly, that many people within the company recognized that the insurance industry in general was going through a period of change, but, more importantly, that they were uncertain about how the Prudential was going to face this change. They were critical of management communication on the subject. Paradoxically, although understandably, the very stability of the company, which made people feel a great deal of pride and interest in it, also led them to feel uncomfortable with change and to a degree complacent about the need for change. To sum up, people were dissatisfied with existing communication practices. Fewer than one-third (30 per cent) of employees agreed that existing channels of communication in the company were good enough.

As a result of the communication audit, employees were told that management was to introduce an action plan. This would include developing and reviewing annually a communication policy and plan within each individual business area; four management reports each year to keep staff informed of plans and activities in the business areas, in the form of videos and printed material as part of a presentation by key managers; training managers throughout the Prudential as 'key communicators' to enable them to take on an effective communication role;

and the establishment of regular monitoring and feedback procedures to ensure staff views were known at the highest level.

When the 1987 communication audit was completed, there was shown to be a distinct improvement in confidence in senior management. Some 76 per cent thought management was doing its best to ensure their future in a difficult economic climate, compared with 64 per cent two years previously. Moreover, 85 per cent thought they were working for a progressive company, compared with 60 per cent in the previous survey.

Those key communicators became a vital part of the internal communication programme when Prudential took a major strategic decision to create a new corporate image, breaking away from its sleeping giant past. The management wanted to demonstrate that while it had a tremendous tradition of service behind it, the company also lived in the present and looked forward to developing ever-widening services to the public in the future. To quote Brian Corby, chief executive: 'The underlying purpose of a new corporate identity is to draw together the diverse strands which make up the Prudential Corporation and to present them under a common banner with a common purpose. The new identity underlies our determination to play a major role in the financial services markets'.

But none of these aims was achievable without having the staff behind them. If the staff were to be the ambassadors of the new corporate image, they had to be convinced of the underlying philosophy which lay behind it. Without that root-and-branch understanding and commitment, the company's new public persona could easily look threadbare in a short passage of time. And the company had the problem – as do many service industries – of getting the message across to staff whose function is out in the field, widely dispersed from the operations at headquarters.

The company has a staff newspaper, issued monthly to some 30,000 staff in the UK and overseas, and a regular programme of quarterly videos to inform staff of important developments. The 450 key communicators are called together on a regular basis and issued with videos and briefing packs, so that when they return to their own base of operation, they can put messages across to staff throughout the country.

The new image concept, however, needed an internal communication operation which was much more dramatic in its impact. The Prudential needed to show it meant business. The launch, both public and to the staff, had to be high profile. It had to be to capture the hearts and minds of the staff. Nine months were spent planning the operation – perhaps not a long time by normal standards, but the aim was to launch before Big Bang in October 1986, the date which would to a large extent symbolize an era of increased activity within the financial service sector.

The new identity launch also went off with a big bang for a week in September. The Royalty Theatre in London was hired and during the period twelve live presentations were made to a total of 8,000 staff – 30 per cent of the United Kingdom workforce, some of whom had never been to London. The remaining staff were given separate presentations by the key communicators. Moreover, a small department was set up in-house to monitor implementation of the identity and to determine staff reactions to the launch. Feedback is as essential to internal communication as imparting the message itself. As a senior practitioner of public relations has been heard to remark more than once, 'Communication within companies can be like the Bermuda Triangle: information can disappear without trace'.

It has a further significance for companies in service industries whose staff come into contact with customers every day of their working lives. As Jan Carlzon, president of Sweden's SAS airline, graphically puts it: 'Each time a member of the staff meets a passenger it is a moment of truth. Either the customer gets a good impression or a bad one'. For British Airways, with 21 million passengers each year, each of whom will come into contact with ten to twenty BA staff on a journey, that is more than 210 million moments of truth each year! That, at least, is how BA's public relations and internal communication departments view the background to their operation: it is part of their *raison d'etre*, which has earned them plaudits for the effort the company puts into its internal communication.

In internal communication, the baggage handler in Djibouti is treated as having the same importance as a senior pilot. Indeed, they could find themselves questioning the same senior manager at one of the customer care and information forums – sessions which can last from one day to a week – which the company runs throughout the year at its Concorde Centre. Staff are flown in regularly from all over the world to participate in these sessions.

But internal communication goes beyond that. BA's newspaper, distributed to its 48,000 staff at home and abroad, is rare: few other companies in the world produce a regular weekly edition. Moreover, a daily bulletin of company news is keyed into the company's main computer, meaning that an estimated 80 per cent of world-wide staff can have access to it on the terminals. In addition, about four times a month, there is a regular managers' brief which contains important company news they have to communicate to staff.

This sophisticated, although admittedly costly, internal communication network not only serves the purpose of maintaining company ethos day by day but can be of immense value when there really is a big event affecting every member of the staff. Nothing could have been more dramatic for British Airways that its privatization: the biggest story in the company's history. It was the subject uppermost in the minds of employees everywhere. It was not something that could be glossed over by the company newspaper; and, as a house journal, it was regarded legally as an official company document. This meant, for the paper's staff, that a new perspective was added to any newspaper's continual need for accuracy.

Michael Blunt, the paper's editor, had to work out with the company's legal director a system enabling the lawyers working on the flotation to check all relevant copy to ensure every item was 100 per cent accurate and that no wrong interpretations could be inferred. This meant at times every line going through five different sets of lawyers – the company's own legal team, their counterparts in Whitehall, the solicitors working for British Airways and the government's merchant banking advisers, and the counsel working on the offer in the United States. On top of this, most stories were also examined minutely by the various groups set up in the airline to handle the privatization, by the company's public affairs director, David Burnside, and often by the chief executive, Sir Colin Marshall.

Not the best – or certainly not the easiest – way of running a weekly newspaper! But its value as a means of communication to employees about what was happening hardly needs stressing. The drama of the story of course is not something with which the average company paper often has to deal, but it does forcibly underline how important newsletters or newspapers can be in communicating to employees what is happening within a company. While a little knowledge may be dangerous, companies must also bear in mind that ignorance is the most insidious destroyer of employee morale.

The privatization of British Airways also brought into play another aspect which should never be left on one side when internal communication is under examination – the growth and use of share option schemes and profit-sharing. These should not be viewed solely as financial transactions. When employees become shareholders in the company they work for, there is an important change in their status. They become members in the full sense, able to vote for (or against) the re-election of directors and on all other matters which under company law must be put to the shareholders. They must be told what is happening to the company. The benefits that accrue both ways are inestimable – a fact, without wishing to be political, which is now dawning upon the trade union movement, where there has been a significant about-face in attitudes to employee shareholding.

Newspapers, videos, information sheets, meetings, all foster an understanding of the role and responsibilities of the individual or the work unit within a company. Equally, they can motivate staff, through giving recognition to their value, and also act as a channel for upward communication, allowing staff to inform senior or middle management of views and attitudes being expressed at lower levels. All these benefits were brought into play in the takeover battle when BTR made a bid for Pilkington Brothers. How Pilkington mobilized the workforce behind it to resist the bid is a classic example of the effectiveness of a carefully planned and deployed internal communication strategy.

In the winter of 1986 life at Pilkington was as no one had known it before. From the moment BTR's bid for the company was announced to the day two months later when it was withdrawn, the company was rarely out of the headlines as one of the most remarkable takeover battles seen in the United Kingdom was fought out. Not surprisingly, the headlines tended to focus on the developments in the City and on the demonstrations mounted by the unions and the local community: the role of the public relations and personnel departments was less in the public eye (a maxim for effective public relations could be that, unlike children, it should be heard but not seen), but just as critical.

The company, in planning its resistance campaign, set out five main objectives: to keep all employees aware of the publicly available information on the bid and to get the latest news to them within half a day of its publication; to be in a position to answer employees' queries and to tell them about their personal situation; to be able to respond quickly to pension enquiries from former employees; to maintain open communication with employee representatives; and to maintain open communication with the local community.

Implementing the strategy, however, was not straightforward. If Pilkington were, as is often supposed, a one-town company, it might have been simple enough, but there is far more to it than St Helens, in Lancashire. Only 6,000 of its 53,000-strong workforce are based there. In the United Kingdom it has 14,000 people working at more than seventy other sites (its biggest plant is in fact in Scotland), and another 39,000 are based overseas, working at twenty-seven locations spread across fifteen countries.

In effect, meeting those objectives – and particularly the first – meant setting up a round-the-clock international news agency, using the combined resources of the public relations and personnel departments. 'We didn't want our employees to have to find out from television what was going on,' recalled John Gillipsie, director of personnel, who spent the entire two months working solely on the campaign.

The main means of achieving that objective was through the company's bulletin system. Normally bulletins are mailed out, but for the duration of the takeover battle all the stops were pulled out to make sure they reached every site within half a day. Where they were available, fax or telex were used; for other sites, delivery was by car or motor-cycle. If all else failed, the contents of the bulletins were dictated over the telephone. To keep up communication with the local community, the company was allowed to designate St Helens town hall as a company site, so that senior councillors could receive news at the earliest opportunity.

At the start of the campaign, Gillipsie and Tony Cove, public relations manager, had met with the personnel directors from each of Pilkington's seven UK divisions and designated them as the contact point for receiving and passing back information. They were asked to arrange for back-ups in case they were not available at any time of the day or night. In addition, they had to appoint one executive at each site to be responsible for receiving and disseminating the information. For overseas sites, two executives responsible for liaison with Europe and the rest of the world were given the same responsibilities.

One factor working in Pilkington's favour was that share movements had given the company a clear early warning of a possible bid, and it was therefore geared up to put the communication system into operation from day one. Thus the first bulletin was rushed out on the same day that the bid was announced (20 November), telling employees of the board's recommendation to shareholders that they should 'treat this misconceived bid with the contempt it deserves'. Between that and the final announcement of victory on 20 January the exercise was repeated whenever there was a significant development.

The communication exercise involved more than the group bulletins, of course. Briefing groups were extended or, where necessary, revived. Five special issues of the group newspaper were produced. A ten-line phone service was installed, and employees, or anyone else, could call to hear a recorded summary of the latest developments; it attracted around 1,000 calls a day. In the head office a news room was set up to display all the published documents, press cuttings and transcripts of television and radio coverage. Copies of cuttings and transcripts – which by the end of the campaign added up to no fewer than 650 pages – were also sent out to every site, and news rooms were set up in some locations.

As an exercise against the clock it proved to be a considerable feat of internal communication, with employees being kept abreast of developments all the time. But, thankfully, the art of good employee communication is not usually driven by such *force majeure* considerations. The need to communicate with staff more effectively has also been dictated by the technological changes which have occurred over the past two decades. Training of staff has had to become more intensive if a company is to be successful and, in turn, there has had to be a more positive approach to internal communication, although these developments are not as widespread as they ought to be in much of the financial sector.

There are now more internal newspapers, newsletters and briefings, all of which has to be to the good, although one can argue about the general level of quality. There has also been an explosion in the non-broadcast corporate sector of film and video production to service expanding internal communication needs, and, as it has grown, so the quality of the visual image has become more important for companies using it. This has been prompted by the realization that no one used to the visual quality of broadcast television will take kindly to a poorly made company programme. In fact quite the reverse: poor production quality could be – in fact almost certainly will be – counter-productive. An employee does not have to be a graduate of a film and television college to know when he or she is being served up a shoddy piece of work.

For some, attitudes towards the use of video are different. Nigel Whittaker of Woolworth, for instance, believes it is limited in its usefulness because the more complex the subject message, the less effective video becomes as a medium. 'Inevitably, because of the nature of the medium, television tends to trivialize', he argues. 'While personal, face-to-face will always be the most effective means of communication, the next best has to be the written word.'

BP, although it uses many other means of communication, such as company-wide publications and management briefs, has made effective use of its quarterly news video for staff. In fact the use of video is increasing in importance within BP as a vehicle of staff communication. It has been producing its quarterly video for the past nine years, featuring major news items and developments from around the group, and including regular interviews with directors and senior managers. The programme has a professional presenter – Brian Redhead – and is circulated to BP's principal locations world-wide for showing to staff. Video is also used by BP's individual businesses to allow senior management to address staff in many different locations on major issues affecting their strategy, organization and operations in what they see as a more personal way than the printed word. However, the company does not regard it as the panacea for all communication needs. David Walton, head of public affairs, strongly argues that its treatment needs to be professional, lively and attractive if it is to win and retain the interest of staff.

In the final analysis, providing high quality employee communication – and using the full range of techniques available today – is a costly exercise. While a company cannot readily gain a precise measure of the value of its communication to its employees, the best endeavour to get some structured feedback through periodic surveys and through advisory groups made up of managers and staff.

Effective employee communication is not achieved overnight. It requires a long-term commitment, both in terms of policy and resources, and a willingness constantly to adapt to the changing communication needs of the organization. Whatever the method, the driving force has to be guided by an overriding principle: a better informed staff will mean a better staff all round.

That may be a truism, but how do you make it come true? Where does one begin improving internal communication? Organizations such as the British Institute of Management and the Industrial Society are good starting points. Both have produced brochures on how best to communicate with employees. BIM, for instance, produces a checklist, too detailed to incorporate here, which shows that those interested in developing better internal communication should be asking these kind of questions:

- What kind of internal communication exists within the various levels of employee in your organization?
- Are meetings or briefing sessions held to communicate policy, progress and problems to employees?
- Does the company inform its employees via a house journal, wall newspapers, notice boards, video or other methods?
- Do all employees receive a copy of the annual report and accounts?
- Does the company give all new employees a comprehensive booklet explaining its operations and setting out their rights and duties?

5

Marketing financial services

Colin Trusler

Over the past few years enormous progress has been made in the acceptance of financial marketing, particularly in the retail sector – banking, building societies, life assurance, unit trusts and the like. But much of this progress has been a surface show of activity rather than a deep-seated management commitment.

When commentators remark on the development of marketing in the 1970s and 1980s, they tend to cite in evidence the rapid rise of advertising expenditure or the proliferation of product introductions. They applaud the greater use of market research to steer and evaluate marketing effort and the widening use of communication media like direct marketing. While this process has indeed taken place, all too often it has been in a strategic vacuum.

What is only now beginning to emerge is a recognition that marketing is an integral part of corporate management, not just a specialist departmental skill, and that the marketing process is concerned with the infinite extension and planned profitability of the corporate life cycle, not merely the development and promotion of products. So, while most financial service companies now acknowledge the importance of marketing, many simply do not know how to make it work. They claim to be market-orientated and to some extent they are right, but if we peep beneath the veneer and analyse how the company puts its act together, the story is often very different.

Far too often we find inadequate market research or market analysis to drive the process, and marketing and sales staff are frequently inadequately trained. Many marketing advances tend to be the result of top management intuition rather than detailed market analysis. The trouble often is not that the consumer is not researched enough or that chief executives instil too strong a profit emphasis, it is because marketing people do not know how to bridge the gap between the two. Of course the task is difficult; consumer needs and corporate profits are often in conflict and hard decisions have to be taken. Nevertheless, creating a dynamic equilibrium between customer needs and profit is the central responsibility of marketing management.

The financial services marketplace, deregulated and increasingly technology-driven, has become turbulent and fiercely competitive. The way for companies to survive and prosper in this environment is to be market-led. That means adopting an operating style which leads directors, management and staff to appreciate that the business exists to serve its customers, and inspires top management to set aside resources for research into customer needs and responses, to develop new products or services to satisfy those needs profitably and to see that customers are told about the company and its services.

Marketing is about profit margins and levels of customer service. It embraces all top management's responsibilities, including the development of the business, investment programmes and acquisition strategies, the allocation of resources, and attitudes to customers, staff, shareholders and society in general.

Directors have a responsibility to define what business they are in. The definitions then need to be communicated to everyone in the company so that they know what the management intends and can ensure that the detailed plans and programmes throughout the company are focused on these objectives.

Marketing cannot flourish without a commitment to change at the top of the company. Business is about the management and marketing of innovation and risk. Innovation is at the heart of marketing management, which should represent the formalized entrepreneurial aim of management.

In this country much of our recent economic history has been characterized by business strategies based upon rationalization, contraction and cost reduction. As a result, many financial service companies are heavily production- or administration-orientated rather than market-orientated. Far too few are organized to achieve rising profits in the 1990s.

So what are the essentials for successful marketing in financial services? They are mainly the qualities that a consumer goods marketeer would recognize and endorse:

1 A premium product range, differentiated by branding.
2 Careful, consistent promotion of the premium values in the brand.
3 A disciplined sales force, supported by an effective management information system.
4 A determined application and combination of skills throughout the company, from board level to front office staff, to serve the customer.

But there is one characteristic of financial service marketing that differentiates it from consumer goods and is fundamental to success. This quality is not so much being *market-led* as being *service-driven*.

At the risk of oversimplifying, we no longer live in a manufacturing economy but a service economy, where 'relationships' are more important than physical products, and where 'long-term relationships' – the buzz phrase of financial service marketeers – replace a deal-orientated, volume-based mentality. This should not be surprising. Over the past twenty years consumption of financial products, whether bank and building society accounts, ownership of shares and equity-related products, or home ownership, has been expanding rapidly. The market penetration strategies that typified financial services in the 1970s – pricing (interest rates) and product diversification – are being replaced by two major forces more suited to the maturing marketplace:

(a) Service marketing, as the quality of the customer's relationship with the company becomes of paramount importance.
(b) Corporate conglomeration, as each player seeks to provide a comprehensive range of products and 'shut out' competitors.

These are likely to be the twin foundations for marketing strategies as financial service companies gear up for the 1990s. Together they raise major new issues for communication and organization structures.

Service marketing in particular will call for a return to the most fundamental principles of leadership and to a rethinking of a company's basic reasons for being. Every time a financial service company does anything for a customer, the latter makes an assessment of the quality of the service, even if unconsciously. The sum of his or her repeated assessments and the collective assessments of all customers establishes the company's image of service quality. This process also takes place in the minds of non-customers of course, because of such stimuli as advertising or press reports.

One of the most valuable uses of market research is to find out as much as possible about customers' needs and perceptions of service. A company can only score consistently highly on service quality if it knows what evaluation factors its customers are applying when they think about it and what it offers. It is no good top management professing a commitment to service quality unless the process is monitored. Without day-by-day vigilance, the quality of service will tend to regress to mediocrity.

To survive and prosper in financial services, the company must show that it has something special to offer. In financial services customers do not readily see important differences in the choices of services offered to them. Service quality, used as part of an added value marketing strategy and clearly articulated, monitored and communicated, can be a very powerful weapon.

To achieve this goal means accepting the fact that, in financial service retailing, employees are the key element in the marketing mix. They are not just the workforce; increasingly they *are* the product. Their training and commitment to customer service will increasingly become the demarcation between the winners and losers in the marketplace.

This is not just a restatement of the old customer satisfaction ratings that have been used for years. One of the most common symptoms of mediocrity in service is when the customer has to run through an organizational maze to get his or her needs met. Banks still fall into this trap at branch level, although much progress has been made; the utilities, some newly privatized, are still among the worst offenders.

In future a breakdown of elitist attitudes and factional interests in financial service companies will be essential. In particular, the commitment to customer service of back office people – accountants, computer specialists and so on – is necessary. This should lead to restructured and streamlined service delivery systems so that customer service is treated with the same degree of precision as product development.

Organizations that have achieved excellence in service are obvious, and their internal characteristics are fairly easy to identify:

- They have a strong vision, based upon a strategy for service that is clearly communicated.
- They practise visible management and talk service routinely.
- They have customer-friendly systems.
- They market their service to customers and, internally, to employees.
- They measure service quality and make the results available to service people.

For all this to happen in financial service companies, it is essential for marketing people to play a leading role in creating and monitoring a service quality system. They must also engage in employee communication, so that staff morale and motivation – the creative energy to perform well – is harnessed to the generation of customer satisfaction.

Corporate conglomeration, the second principal characteristic of financial service marketing, is producing an ever-widening product range to choose from. Conglomeration has taken many forms in recent years, as banks, building societies and insurance companies have penetrated each other's markets and acquired or developed competitive capabilities, such as fund management houses or chains of estate agents. Even the clearing banks' monopoly of money transmission, while still substantially intact, has been breached by the building societies. In the 1990s the effective differences, in product terms, between these institutions will become more apparent than real.

Since a good deal of resources and creative energy has gone into the product development process, the leaders and laggards are now broadly level, supported by a degree of technology which in most cases has parallel potential for marketing purposes. The banks, in particular, are now competitively interfaced in all markets. As everyone recognizes that the advantage of being first to launch a new service is usually very short-term, the search for superiority is taking on new forms.

Major efforts are now being made to break down the two principal weaknesses inherent in conglomeration: data incompatibility and fragmentation of image.

In most instances in the hierarchy of choices, the key brand is the company itself. For most people, financial services are a marginal part of their lives, a small part of their attention span. Financial products tend to be similar. So the competitive noise is deafening; and, compounding all this, the diversity of media choice is growing fast.

The result is that people buy companies rather than products. They feel certain companies are 'more for them' than others. Providing there is no practical discord, such as pricing disparities (and even these are balanced with other qualities, like service), they will act on this preference. But their feel is vulnerable to experience of the company as manifested in branch offices, correspondence or other forms of contact. It is a primary job of marketing in financial services to ensure that all these contacts produce customer satisfaction. Nowhere is this more essential than in customer communications.

All communication – whether advertising, brochures, merchandising, direct marketing, technology, sales – should be driven by a clear, consistent strategy, irrespective of market segmentation and product differences. Unless all communication is grafted harmoniously and coherently to the central identity of the company, it can backfire or fail to be effective.

Corporate communication can be defined as the job of marketing the whole company, rather than its products. This is the paramount task for service companies in today's market conditions.

Most of the data bases supporting the operations of financial service companies originated from the move to computerization in the 1960s and 1970s, when the management objective rarely encompassed the customer. Now the process is being revised, as management demands information to enable it to plan, monitor and market the business. Customer information is seen as the key that can break down the walls between profit centres and business units in financial conglomerates (at least, where conflicts of interest do not arise). Only knowledge about the customer base can make it a manageable entity, to which differing group products can be sold in a continuous process through the life cycle of the customer.

Translating a financial database into a customer information system, however, is expensive and the implications complex. Not many will embark on the process; fewer will complete it successfully. But the marketing benefits, in strategic terms, will be very powerful; companies with customer information systems will reach markets others will not be able to enter. Information technology will become an inherent part of the product range of the future – a far cry from the crude first generation offerings such as Prestel and home banking. But all will have, explicitly or implicitly, the same goal: the satisfaction of customer needs on a value-for-money, convenient basis, often in the home.

Many of the current pressures in the marketplace – product development, information technology, conglomeration – are having a negative impact on marketing effectiveness. They are fragmenting the image of the providers and weakening the potential implicit in brand marketing.

The notion of what constitutes a brand in financial service marketing is a much debated and ultimately irresolvable issue. Is the brand the product, or the product group, or the delivery system, or the whole company? Or a combination of all of these?

Communication must be co-ordinated to be effective. Co-ordination means channelling the creative energies of the organization – externally and internally – in a way that supports and enhances corporate strategy.

All too frequently companies speak with one voice in advertising, contradict themselves in their personal selling activities, deny themselves in their direct marketing and then muddle the whole process with their product and customer service policy. Under the skin they become two animals – or more. Through the diversity of their communication, they confuse and alienate people, rather than persuading and attracting them. This is not a simple matter of tidy-mindedness; it puts a finger on corporate schizophrenia, a condition that over time can become terminal.

The message is a simple one. As life becomes more complicated and competitive, a coherent communication policy becomes crucial for market acceptance and profitable growth. This message is relatively new to financial services, where marketing is a recent arrival.

While customer orientation is the only approach that makes sense in a competitive world, coherent communication also requires total planning and co-ordination; it must encompass the whole company. It can be an expensive mistake to assume that only the customer matters. Any successful organization needs effective responses from groups other than customers; its corporate communication programme must therefore embrace other key groups, such as employees, the media, suppliers, government and shareholders.

Total communication should be designed to give a consistent impression. That much abused phrase 'corporate image' is a vast idea, and the problems of implementing it can be daunting.

Everything must be co-ordinated to put over one simple and persuasive story. Otherwise it will be very difficult to penetrate the colossal curtain of competitive noise that surrounds the customer. As Ted Levitt once said: 'He'll switch off his hearing aid'.

But how do you know if he is interested in listening to what you have to say in the first place?

The task of satisfying consumer demand today is much more difficult than it used to be. Customers constantly seek greater choice. They look for the best price. They demand better service. The paradox is that they want greater specialization yet greater simplicity at the same time. Who can blame them?

How far then can we identify customer needs through research? How successful is research in identifying needs and helping management relate them to the introduction of new products or services? The answer is that, although research can play a valuable part in helping management refine its marketing policies, it makes only a modest contribution to the creation of marketing strategies.

Demography and life-style analyses have been valuable in spotting market opportunities for asset management among older, high net worth individuals. But average consumers find it difficult, if not impossible, to conceptualize or articulate their needs for financial services beyond basic levels.

When asked about their needs, most people express them in simple, mechanical terms: cheapest loans, highest rate deposits, both with instant accessibility; secure, high growth unit trusts; omniscient bank managers. All are the programmed reactions of the under-informed, uninterested consumer. This situation is changing but slowly.

Another failing in the use of market research is that so much is ad hoc and focused on a specific problem or task. Rarely do research findings get merged into a database. This means that defining market segments, which is central to marketing strategy, is difficult or impossible.

But the days of the so-called mass market are at an end, which means it is essential to target the marketing effort and concentrate marketing resources and budgets. Segmentation drives this whole process, but can easily be dominated by statistical techniques – which will only confuse, not clarify, marketing choices. Here are eight pitfalls in segmentation:

1 Segmentation by product, not by market.
2 Following competitor segmentation – stultifying innovation.
3 Demographic segmentation – tells you nothing about the underlying reasons people use your company and its products.
4 Relying on a single segment – oversimplifying the process of motivation.
5 Applying too many criteria – leading to unmanageable complexity.

6 Developing segmentation schedules that cannot be implemented. Each scheme must drive a marketing programme.
7 Putting priority on the largest segment – a 'lemming strategy' where competitors converge..
8 Failing to assess comparative profitability of segments before selection – a self-targeted missile that can strike an organization square on its bottom line.

The best approach will depend largely on the nature of the financial services company, but one that should be considered is building a flexible marketing model in which behavioural, attitudinal and profit-related data are combined. The benefit of this is threefold:

(a) Segments can be defined in terms of profit potential.
(b) Products and service levels can be planned to meet the potential of each major segment.
(c) The effectiveness of communication with each segment can be maximized.

All this data needs to be analysed and the conclusions that flow from it applied. Which leads to a third component in the formulation of marketing policies: the competition. Marketing is about competitiveness as much as customer satisfaction or profitability. The objective of research and segmentation is the creation of a competitive strategy for the organization. This should result from the corporate strategy and be programmed in the annual marketing plan.

Corporate strategy gives a focus to the organization and defines its purpose. Management strategies find many forms, but increasingly financial organizations are trying to do two things: create and communicate competence in their defined business areas, and then compete through differentiation. This combination determines product, portfolio, pricing and distribution decisions. Each company's unique positioning results from how it resolves the following sum:

Who are we?

+

What do people want?

Segmentation is central to providing the answer, by identifying the differences that drive consumers and the differences that create profit and loss.

The analysis should focus on fundamentals. What is our role? What are we good at? How do we make our money? What return must we make to fulfil our plans? Where is the market going? What are the segments for today, for tomorrow? How do we organize ourselves for effective delivery?

Given the increasing polarization between a high price/superior service company and a low cost provider of basic services, the choices are getting more difficult, particularly as it is difficult to play the middle of the market.

Once you have determined your target markets, assisted by your segmentation, how do you define the competitive position of your company, or your product range? Here are three useful techniques.

1 *Customer need analysis.* A simple matrix to help identify the distinctive benefits that your customers purchase from you. Simply define the main segments and summarize their main needs – a simple process in concept, but difficult to do well. For each segment concentrate on only three or four benefits – the 'jugular' issues that really matter.

2 *Corporate benefit analysis.* Use a matrix to assess your main products against your customers' primary needs. Give them some kind of ranking. Be realistic and base your assessment not just on what the product does, but what performance it is perceived to have.

3 *Competitor analysis.* Use a matrix to profile the main competitor products and compare and contrast them with your own; highlight the differences and relate them to your product benefit analysis. This is harder to do but it will lead to a convergence of customer and competitor analysis. It will also define your market position. If it is the result of rigorous analysis based on hard data, the result will tell you where you need to improve your product offering, both against competition and on behalf of the customer.

In today's environment for financial services, it is part of the marketing man's responsibility to challenge the conventional wisdom of the organization to ensure its efficiency in the marketplace. Marketing is well placed to see gaps in the market and opportunities for new products based upon developing technology. Despite the competition, there is an immense volume of business to be done, but only the most market-orientated firms will achieve their goals profitably.

However, a word of warning! The concept of 'narrow band' marketing, reflected in rigid product management structures or too strict observance of segmentation policies, can fragment the identity of a company and weaken its ability to compete. This is a message for chief executives, who, usually alone, have the power to dictate and enforce communication policies.

As David Bernstein has said:

Images are powerful. A company is what people feel it is, believe it is, as much as what they know it is. The company has to know how it is perceived. It has to be in charge of its image. To a chief executive suspicious of slogans and simplistic solutions, I say: people sum you up in a few words. The least you can do is do it for them.

So what can be done to move the company towards this position? How do you start? The following points give some guidance:

1 Clarify where you want to go. Choose the image factors that matter in your business, relate them to your company, discuss them with your colleagues and put them into a form of words that is understandable by all, particularly employees. The words must be related to your business, achievable and with a competitive cutting edge. This is your mission statement, which, when realized, can make the difference between 'business as usual' and a leadership position in your market.

2 Establish where you are. The company philosophy should help identify the important dimensions on which the company should be judged. Check these out with key audiences, remembering that customers are only one of several important groups. Use techniques such as corporate benefit analysis and competitive ranking to locate the company in the marketplace. Research is necessary to make sure this objective reflects external perceptions and benefits, not corporate introspection.

3 Confront your plan with the results of your research. How close is the fit? What has to be done to close the gaps? Are the differences to do with performance or perception? Is it a product or a communication problem? Are there different problems in different areas or with different audiences? (Yes, almost certainly!)

4 Isolate the communication tasks. Firstly check how, and how well, you communicate with your main audiences. Are your communications planned or incidental, direct or indirect? Do you use the most effective media? Do your messages relate to your central philosophy? Are they tailored to public perceptions and prejudices, or are you just using a loudhailer?

5 Programme your communication activity. The object of segmentation is to achieve cost-effective delivery of benefits. The same is true for communication: depending on their knowledge and use of the company, different groups will have varying information needs. You should therefore have a programme for each without, however, forgetting the need for consistency in all communication.

6 Lastly, remember that communication is not a management tool unless it is controlled. Only research can ensure this. Data is a basic requirement of communication planning and evaluation. Time and time again companies ignore this simple truth.

The concept of corporate communication is large, the notion of image somewhat vaporous. But the importance of image cannot be denied, since it reflects actuality – actual experience of companies, actual knowledge of them, actual feelings, beliefs and impressions. Every company has an image, whether it likes it or not. The only choice is whether it is one that is good for business or not. And it is a real choice.

A company *can* assess its image and manage it as part of its strategic management process. The result is a contribution to the whole enterprise, making it more productive and more profitable.

6

Regulation of the financial services industry

Betty Powell

All sectors of the financial services industry now appear to appreciate the importance of corporate communication – all forms of public relations, exhibitions, design and marketing, including direct mail and especially advertising. Use of, and expenditure on, these techniques have grown enormously over recent years and as yet shows no sign of having reached a peak.

For those public relations practitioners prepared and able to familiarize themselves with the demands of the Financial Services Act 1986 (FSA) and its contingent regulatory system, many opportunities are created. Although the legal responsibility for complying with the legislation rests for the most part with the employer or client, companies will appreciate those professionals able to save them time and money by knowing enough about, say, the advertising rules to avoid the creation of campaigns which breach those rules or proposals which bring non-investment firms within the scope of the Act.

As an added advantage, any such practitioners would then also understand enough about the Act and its workings to stop themselves being persuaded, though unintentionally, into illegal activities.

What were the motives underlying the reform of the legislative framework? There had been a series of financial scandals where private investors had lost money; the single most important piece of existing legislation (The Prevention of Fraud (Investments) Act 1958) was outdated and inadequate; other regulatory legislation was piecemeal and somewhat ramshackle. The Conservative government's philosophy of encouraging a wider proportion of the United Kingdom population to invest, particularly in shares, meant that investment vehicles had to be made both more accessible and more reliably run. Financial markets were increasingly operating on a world-wide basis and, with London bidding to be one of the top three with New York and Tokyo, there was concern that London's reputation should not be tarnished by corruption or inadequacy.

The resulting Financial Services Act 1986 provides the basis on which a regulatory framework has been erected to meet these needs. The Act defines the investments to be regulated (Schedule I), which means in effect all financial investments with the exception of traditional banking and building society business and the money markets. So included are shares, securities, commodity and financial futures and options, and collective investment schemes (unit trusts and long-term life assurance come into it too). Direct investment in 'physicals' such as gold, diamonds and stamps is not included, but the government can widen or narrow the definition by order if necessary.

The Financial Services Act lays down a framework for regulation of both organizations and concepts, and gives power to the Secretary of State for Trade and Industry. It is then up to the Secretary of State when and to what extent he delegates these powers to the designated agency, the Securities and Investments Board (SIB).

The primary concept on which the regulatory system is based is that of authorization: every investment firm needs to be authorized in order to continue trading. The unauthorized carrying on of investment business – and the legislation gives a very wide definition of what that is – becomes a criminal offence punishable by two years' imprisonment or an unlimited fine. So it is particularly important that public relations consultants should not, say, when undertaking a direct mail operation behave in such a way that their own activities come within the scope of that definition.

There are two clauses in the Act's definition of investment business to be considered here: 'making or offering or agreeing to make arrangements for buying, selling or subscribing for or underwriting investments' and 'giving or offering or agreeing to give to persons in their capacity as investors or potential investors advice on the merits of their purchasing, selling or subscribing for or underwriting an investment' (Schedule I, clauses 13 and 15). Consultants should ensure that at all times they are acting as the agent of the investment firm and not independently when doing anything which could be construed as coming within the definition of carrying on investment business.

The other danger to which public relations firms should be alert is to clients that are companies, or perhaps charities, which do not themselves carry on investment business but may offer their mailing lists and perhaps name to an investment firm for a fee. Such arrangements need to be examined very rigorously in order to avoid inadvertent entry into the investment arena by the client.

In order to obtain authorization, a firm has to be 'fit and proper', that is, of good repute, competent to do the type of investment business for which it is applying for authorization and with sufficient finance to support its operations. Once authorized, a firm is required to make regular financial returns to its regulatory body and is subject to spot checks. Besides meeting the specific requirements to obtain authorization, a firm once authorized is then subject to detailed conduct-of-business rules, covering such areas as independence, product bias, excessive charges, churning (advising a client to sell existing investments and buy others at very frequent intervals in order to boost commission earned), twisting (advertising one product in order to then sell another), knowing your customer, customer agreements, best advice, disclosure of material interest, appointed representatives, advertising, cold calling and cancellation.

The regulatory structure created under the FSA has at its peak the Securities and Investments Board, a company limited by guarantee whose board – a mixture of eminent investment practitioners, businessmen and consumer representatives – is appointed by the Secretary of State for Trade and Industry and the Governor of the Bank of England. The SIB's staff is recruited from government service and the investment industry and it also has a high proportion of industry secondees. It is, uniquely for a regulatory body, entirely financed by the industry which it regulates, over which it has a levying power. Because the SIB can offer authorization to firms directly itself, its rulebook covers all types of investment business, the structure closely reflecting the concepts and principles of the Act.

In order that the rules should not be so over-protective as to be counter-productive and thus drive investment firms out of business or overseas, the rulebook is subject to regular examination by the Director-General of Fair Trading. If he identifies any rules which he believes are anti-competitive, as he did with the SIB's policy on polarization and the Life Assurance and Unit Trust Regulatory Organization's commissions agreement, this is reported to the Secretary of State, who then decides whether the rules are necessary for the protection of investors.

However, despite this procedure the initial SIB rulebook has been criticized for being overdetailed and the SIB is in the process of rewriting the rules in a clearer, more accessible and effective way. The recast rules take the form of, first, the general principle involved which will help promote understanding of the objectives and the spirit of the rules. This is followed by the individual rules written in a more straightforward way. It is hoped that this new, clearer style will be adopted by other parts of the regulatory system.

The demands of democracy are met by the SIB making an annual report to the Secretary of State, which he lays before Parliament.

Two areas where the new system will especially benefit investors are in the creation of an industry-wide compensation scheme and in the way in which complaints are dealt with. Before the FSA there were compensation schemes affecting some limited sectors. The Stock Exchange had a discretionary scheme and insurance companies were covered by the Policyholders Protection Act; elsewhere there was nothing. The investors compensation scheme set up by the SIB is run by Investors Compensation Scheme Ltd. It comes into effect only when a firm goes into liquidation and there are insufficient funds to pay the private investors. Under the scheme an investor can claim up to 100 per cent of the first £30,000 lost and 80 per cent of the next £20,000, with a ceiling for each investor of £48,000. It is paid for by the investment industry.

All authorized firms now have a responsibility to deal properly with complaints from investors and to keep adequate records. This was not the case before. The regulatory bodies have to ensure that this is done and also to provide for the investigation of any complaints made to them by dissatisfied investors.

The other parts of the regulatory structure can be divided into three areas: the Self-Regulating Organizations (SROs), the Recognized Professional Bodies (RPBs) and the Recognized Investment Exchanges (RIEs).

The SROs at the time of writing comprise five organizations whose members make up the bulk of Britain's investment industry. They are roughly activity-based organizations, financed and run by their members, whose rules have to provide an equivalent degree of investor protection to the SIB's own rulebook. Their rules must also, like those of the SIB, be acceptable to the Director-General of Fair Trading on competition grounds. They have been recognized by the SIB, which now has the responsibility of ensuring that they regulate their members according to these rules without subjecting them to such detailed supervision as to remove their autonomy.

The five SROs are:

1   *Association of Futures Brokers and Dealers* (AFBD), which regulates firms which carry on business in connection with dealing and arranging and advising on deals in futures, options and contracts for differences, and with investment management of futures, options and contracts for differences portfolios. It has around 400 members.

2   *Investment Management Regulatory Organization* (IMRO), whose member firms engage in investment management, where this is the sole or main activity of the firm or where the member firm describes itself as offering discretionary management services distinct from other activities; management and operation of collective investment schemes; investment management of investment trusts; acting as a trustee of regulated collective investment schemes (such as authorized unit trusts); in-house pension fund management; and investment advice to institutional or other corporate customers. There are around 1,000 members.

3 *Financial Intermediaries, Managers and Brokers Regulatory Association* (FIMBRA), which is for the independent financial adviser. Its members' main activity is advising on and arranging deals in life assurance, in authorized unit trusts and other collective investment schemes; providing investment advisory and management services to retail customers; and advising on and arranging deals in securities (but not as their main activity). Membership is about 10,000.

4 *Life Assurance and Unit Trust Regulatory Organization* (LAUTRO), which regulates for the most part only the retail marketing of life assurance and authorized unit trusts. Authorization is given by the DTI to insurance companies, a power which cannot under European Community law be delegated to the SIB, and unit trusts are authorized by the SIB itself, so LAUTRO is not concerned with the fitness and properness of its members, which includes such matters as their financial standing. The membership is about 400.

5 *The Securities Association* (TSA), the activities of whose members include dealing and arranging deals in shares, debentures, government and other public securities, warrants, certificates representing securities, rights and interests in securities, and futures and options in securities and on foreign exchange. In addition, as a subsidiary matter, it advises on deals in investments, with managing such investments and arranging and advising on transactions in life assurance and collective investment schemes. There are about 900 members.

The RPBs are intended to regulate those individuals whose main activity is the conduct of a profession but who also undertake some investment business. Each professional body itself already regulates its members in the conduct of their professional activities, and their existing rulebooks have been extended to deal with the investment part of that business. The responsibility of the SIB in recognizing an RPB is to ensure that investors are provided with an equivalent degree of investor protection whether an investor goes to a member of an SRO or an RPB.

The Act allows members of an RPB to undertake up to 50 per cent of their activities as investment business and still fall to be regulated by their professional body. Above that level the firm must obtain authorization from the appropriate SRO. However, most professional bodies decided to set a much lower limit to the investment business of their members in order to reduce the regulatory demands laid upon them by the SIB. The SIB's policy is to relate the degree of regulation an RPB must exercise upon its members' investment business to the type and degree of investment business they are permitted to conduct.

Members of RPBs cannot undertake the full range of investment activities permitted by the FSA; those activities calling for greater financial resources and supervision than can be expected in the RPB arena are restricted to members of the appropriate SRO. For example, making a market in shares is permitted only for members of the TSA or those authorized by the SIB.

The RPBs are:

The Law Society of England and Wales
The Law Society of Scotland
The Law Society of Northern Ireland
The Institute of Chartered Accountants in England and Wales
The Institute of Chartered Accountants of Scotland
The Institute of Chartered Accountants in Ireland
The Chartered Association of Certified Accountants
The Institute of Actuaries
The Insurance Brokers Registration Council

As with the SROs, the SIB has the responsibility of ensuring that the RPBs regulate their members according to their rules.

The RIEs are the exchanges themselves. In order to protect investors and conduct business efficiently it is not enough merely to regulate the practitioner's relations with his clients. The actual working of the market itself must be orderly, proper records must be kept and a way provided for complaints to be pursued. Exchanges do not have to be recognized, but any authorized firm dealing on an unrecognized exchange will have to report full details of every deal to its SRO or the SIB.

Some RIEs are:

Baltic Futures Exchange
International Petroleum Exchange
International Stock Exchange
London Futures and Options Exchange
London International Financial Futures Exchange
London Metal Exchange
London Commodity Exchange

The other responsibility passed to the new regulatory system is that of regulating collective investment schemes, including unit trusts. The FSA established an entirely new statutory framework for them, calling for detailed regulations on many matters which previously existed without codified and published rules. The SIB has assumed the responsibility formerly exercised by the DTI of authorizing unit trusts. It is an offence to promote a scheme to the public unless it is an authorized unit trust or is in accordance with very restricted provisions laid down in regulations. The SIB maintains a register of all authorized and recognized unit trust schemes (including overseas schemes permitted to be marketed in the UK).

Promoting an unauthorized investment firm will cause a public relations practitioner to commit a criminal offence, so it is clearly essential to know how to determine whether a firm is or is not authorized. The rules demand that all authorized firms state the fact and give the name of their authorizing body; further, claiming to be authorized when you are not is also a criminal offence. However, merely asking a firm whether or not it is authorized is unlikely to be considered a sufficient verification procedure to protect a consultancy.

The SIB has the responsibility of making information available about authorization and has compiled and keeps up to date a central register in the form of a computerized list of all authorized firms. Access is available via Prestel for a fee of 85p an enquiry, by writing to the SIB or calling on a special telephone number: 01-929 3652.

The SIB's Prestel pages also contain a brief description of the new regulatory system, publications available from the SIB and summaries of any recent announcements made by the SIB, SROs and RPBs.

Increasingly, investment business is crossing national boundaries, and the creation of the European Community internal market in 1992 will quicken this trend. Because of this, overseas firms wishing to market in the UK are seeking the promotional assistance of British public relations consultants.

The FSA makes important changes in the way in which overseas long-term life assurance products and collective investment schemes (unit trusts) are treated. In the past, for example, some Channel Islands and Isle of Man schemes could be marketed in the UK because they were companies listed at the Stock Exchange. This route is no longer open.

Under the Act overseas collective investment schemes have three, and long-term life assurance products two, routes by which to make themselves legally marketable to the UK general public. A collective investment scheme must either be based in a member state of the European Community and have notified the SIB that it intends to be marketed in the UK (section 86) or come from a territory or country designated by the Secretary of State for Trade and Industry (section 87). Such designation is only given to countries which have legislation providing an equivalent level of investor protection to that of the UK, and the SIB must be informed that it is intended to market the scheme in the UK; or, if from neither a member state nor a designated country, the scheme must be approved in its own right (section 88) and to do so must demonstrate that it provides the investor protection lacking in its legal environment.

Long-term life assurance products may obtain access to the UK public by the first two routes mentioned above (section 130), but not the third.

The names of all overseas collective investment schemes able to be marketed in the UK to the general public and long-term life assurance companies able to market their products in the UK can be found in special sections of the central register maintained by the SIB.

Although these products can be marketed in the UK to the general public under the FSA, this does not mean that in every case the companies themselves can market their products, unless they are actually authorized in the UK. For example, some overseas groups have set up separate marketing companies in the UK which have authorization.

European Community companies can market their products directly in the UK, but they must decide whether to be regulated by the SIB or LAUTRO, which will determine whose marketing rules they follow.

The products mentioned above when coming from designated territories or individually approved companies can be legally marketed in the UK. However, firms in these categories must decide whether to do this via a UK authorized firm or whether to do this directly. For direct marketing they must become authorized by becoming members of LAUTRO or be directly authorized by SIB. Products from undesignated countries, not members of the Community and not specifically approved, can be drawn to the attention of authorized persons and some other limited categories of person, but not to the general public.

A totally new area of vital importance to public relations practitioners is the financial advertising rules. These rules are important because they are of a very different character from almost every other method of regulating advertising. Apart from the advertising rules made under the Consumer Credit Act, all other restrictions on advertising are codes of practice.

Firstly, the Financial Services Act itself has a considerable impact. The effect of section 57, which states that investment advertisements must be approved by an authorized person, is not restricted to advertisements issued by members of the investment industry. It affects all investment advertisements but a few exceptions, mostly those advertisements required by law. So, for example, an advertisement featuring a non-financial company's half-yearly figures with comments from the managing director could be caught. For agencies this could mean co-ordinating advertisements with a company's accountants or solicitors, since they are most likely to be the only authorized persons associated with such companies. If this section is breached, a criminal offence is committed, the prosecuting authority being the Department of Trade and Industry.

The definition of investment advertisements is broad, including direct mail, newspapers and magazines, radio and television; the position of promotional press releases is undetermined at the time of writing but they *could* be caught. If unauthorized persons issue investment advertisements, they are guilty of a criminal offence punishable by up to two years' imprisonment and/or an unlimited fine. If anyone in the course of business other than investment business issues an advertisement on the order of another person believing them to be authorized, they will have to show that they had reasonable grounds for this belief and also for the belief that the contents of the advertisement had been approved by an authorized person.

Contravention could mean that any agreements entered into following the advertisement could not be enforced and the other party entitled to recover any money paid plus damages. The potential problem here for agencies is that, for example in direct mail, a lack of research could mean that the 'reasonable grounds' defence could not be used. Merely accepting an individual's word that he was authorized would not be accepted as 'reasonable grounds'.

Financial services firms are both subject to section 57 and the advertising rules of the body which authorizes them. The rules drawn up by the SIB, SROs and RPBs also have the force of law, which means that if a breach causing damage to an investor occurs, it could cause the authorized firm not only to be disciplined but also, more importantly, sued by the private investor himself or by the SIB on the investor's behalf.

If a private investor is sold an investment in breach of the advertising rules and suffers as a result, perhaps because he was misled about the degree of risk, he can go to the courts and claim damages solely on the breach of the rules. Furthermore the advertising rules made under the Act have priority over other organizations' rules, and responsibilities exercised under these rules by the SIB and SRO cannot be delegated. This means that even if a television advertisement has been approved by the television authorities, the originating company is not immune from disciplinary or legal action. However, the rules should not appear too unfamiliar to practitioners, since their origins lie in existing codes, such as the British Code of Advertising Practice.

The rules seek to avoid the issue of advertisements by unauthorized persons by requiring that every advertisement should be approved by an authorized person. Investment firms must have a person whose responsibility this is, and who will keep records of advertisements approved. Before accepting advertisements newspapers must assure themselves that they have been approved by an authorized person and must make an independent check on the SIB's central register to verify the claim of authorization.

Although the SIB and the SROs have similar advertising rules, they are not identical. Advertisements have to follow the rules of the SRO to which the authorized firm placing the advertisement belongs. Their contents must be accurate and relevant (not, for example, misusing graphs or charts to compare the performance of completely different products, or massaging statistics to avoid bad periods) and, where appropriate, contain clear visible warnings about the risks associated with the product, such as volatility or unmarketability.

Advertisements are required generally to indicate who regulates the firm placing the advertisement, so that customers will know to whom complaints should be addressed. The severity of the application of these principles varies according to the form of advertisement – the simplest requirements being for advertisements which carry little or no message (for example, generic advertisements publicizing the name of the company, not a product, do not even need the name of the regulator), and the most severe for advertisements seeking money 'off the page'. Finally advertisements have to be appropriate to the degree of sophistication of those to whom they are directed.

The views expressed in this chapter are those of the author and not necessarily those of the SIB.

7

The ethical jungle

John Hollis

There has never been a time when what is now known as the financial services industry has not been the object of public criticism and distaste. It has had a bad press since Roman times, when the triumvir Crassus founded his fortunes by running the only efficient fire service in Rome and instructing them to stand by idle until he had negotiated a good price with the owner of the blazing building. Some marine salvage operators today follow much the same technique, as do many American lawyers.

Shakespeare's *Merchant of Venice* is the classic expression of the contrast between strictly commercial values and more widely accepted moral principles, as it is of much else that concerns the evolution of financial markets.

For many years now the markets in London and elsewhere have been aware that they operate in what is basically a critical, if not hostile, environment and have accordingly sought to present themselves as providing a service responsibly conducted in the public interest as well as in the interest of the participants. Where monopolies are defended, they are defended on the ground that they are enlightened cartels whose restrictive practices are designed for the protection of their customers.

It has to be said that there is often a good deal of justice in this claim. The Stock Exchange's code of conduct for directors of listed companies, the Takeover Panel's regulations regarding conduct and disclosure, and the Stock Exchange compensation fund have all been initiatives taken by the City authorities themselves to protect the City's own good name and justify its claim to regulate its own affairs. On some issues the City has even been prepared to demand the support of the law to strengthen its hand. It was the Stock Exchange that first demanded that insider trading be made an offence under the law in the, perhaps mistaken, belief that this would help root out the problem. There could be no greater contrast with the outrage of the Football Association when the police intervene to bring charges for criminal assault against players guilty of violent conduct on the field.

In spite of this enlightened attitude, events at Lloyd's in particular and among certain fringe financial services businesses, often only remotely connected with the City and the main financial markets, have led to a new era. Now the regulation of conduct has become a matter for government and the law, or rules made under the law.

One common thread that ran through the lengthy debates in Parliament on the Financial Services Act was that virtually every spokesman opened by paying tribute to the good reputation and high standards of conduct of the City and then proceeded to demand the imposition of rules and restrictions to limit and direct the manner in which the City should be regulated in future. Only Lord Lever in the House of Lords, in a typically robust intervention, poured scorn on the popular misconception that the banking community in London is infested with dangerous criminals. Others justified the apparent conflict between their appreciation of the City's achievements in the field of self-regulation and their demand for the imposition of external regulation by pointing to the likelihood that the breakdown of the traditional frontiers between different functions in the capital markets would also lead to a breakdown in the informal system of checks and balances inherent in the separation of function.

The truth of the matter is that there is a built-in antipathy between those concerned with government, particularly as it affects economic management, and between the financial markets, which are often the most trenchant critics of public economic policy and who by their market reactions often are capable of exposing the folly and frustrating the purposes of government. This antipathy crosses party boundaries. The Conservative Chancellor of the Exchequer, Nigel Lawson, one of the most consistent advocates of market forces, reacted with fury and incomprehension to the world-wide market collapse of 19 October 1987.

In Britain, however, the markets have learned to live with the fact that on one side of the political divide stands a party that is in principle opposed to the capitalist system of which the financial markets form a central part. This is not so in other countries. In America there is a consistent thread of agrarian populism which regards the workings of the financial markets with suspicion but stops short of questioning the underlying principle. In Japan, where there is close informal co-operation between the economic authorities and the markets, which found its most recent expression in the concerted support of share prices following the October 1987 collapse, the harmony between markets and government is almost complete.

This antipathy between government, which seeks to control the economy, and markets, which are fundamentally uncontrollable in their ability to pass judgement on policy and to modify its effects, though irrelevant to the question of how markets should be regulated, inevitably colours the attitudes of politicians when discussing this separate issue.

At the same time this is not an issue that carries any great political sex appeal. It may be sufficient to provide a hobbyhorse on which an individual back-bencher may ride but it is not a weighty enough issue in the public eye to form part of a major platform. It was notable that even after the publicity and controversy attending the passing of the Financial Services Act into law, coupled with the eruption of the Guinness affair into the courts, the Opposition made barely a mention of City regulation in the June 1987 election campaign.

No doubt this reticence was partly due to the facts that the government had taken somewhat precipitate steps to bring forward the Securities and Investments Board's formal recognition, overruling the Office of Fair Trading's reservations, and that the first Guinness arrests had been made and duly televised. These events had to some extent drawn the sting from anything the Opposition might otherwise have wished to say. Nevertheless it remains true that defects in the National Health Service are a far more emotive issue in electoral terms than defects in the supervision of financial markets.

An odd feature of the relationship between politicians and the City is that, however great the antipathy of principle between the two camps, it remains true that those caught in financial scandals or misbehaviour have often been those financiers or businessmen who, at any rate before their exposure, commanded the admiration and attention of the political leaders of the day. This is not to say that political figures have been directly implicated in recent scandals, only that they are capable of considerable naivety in their associations with those whom they view as powerful and influential in business affairs.

Those who would attempt to devise and impose legal constraints, sub-statutory regulations or codes of ethical behaviour in the field of financial services, whether from within the industry or from without, are faced with the difficulty of determining what should be the conceptual basis upon which these regulations are framed. It is often said that the driving forces in financial markets, as indeed in other forms of economic activity, are greed and fear. Neither are ethical concepts.

Economic motivation is essentially based on self-interest, although there is a powerful argument that, in the longer view, unless this is diluted by a measure of collective responsibility so that it becomes enlightened self-interest, it is self-destructive. That is essentially the case for self-appointed regulators when justifying their actions and their authority to those they regulate. A market so predatory in its behaviour that it consumes or alienates its customers can only have a short life, however merry.

An outside regulator seeking to impose standards of conduct must, however, find a different philosophical base. This task is made no easier by the fact that judgements on what is or is not acceptable practice are essentially relative. There are no absolute standards of what is or is not accepted market practice, although few would deny that broader standards of general morality should apply.

This is most clearly seen by contrasting the different views of what is acceptable practice in Britain and the United States, most notably in the field of mergers and acquisitions. The British rules, as incorporated in the Takeover Code, are designed above all else to ensure equality of treatment for all concerned shareholders. Bids in excess of 30 per cent of the target company necessarily trigger a mandatory offer on the best terms for the whole of the balance. America, by contrast, takes the view that a major stake may validly be acquired at a premium price and there is no obligation to offer the same terms (or indeed any terms) for the balance. The analogy advanced is that of the piecemeal sale of a block of apartments, where each owner secures the best price available for himself and has no obligation to insist on the same terms for his neighbours.

Similar examples may be found in the practice of a company buying its own shares, which in the United Kingdom was until recently virtually prohibited and is still hedged about with restrictions, while in the US it has long been normal practice and is viewed as a legitimate manoeuvre. The preservation of the rights of pre-emption of existing shareholders, which has recently been the subject of much controversy, is yet another case in point; the American system of issuing and distributing secondary issues for cash has never allowed existing shareholders such pre-emptive rights.

Nor can any firm basis for ethical standards, as opposed to observance of the letter of the law, be found in statutory regulations or the various levels of rules and codes of conduct which derive from them. Since April 1988, if two individuals, waiting for the fairway to clear so that they can begin a round of golf, choose to while away an idle moment discussing their investments or their life assurance policies and one gives the other advice, a criminal offence will have been committed unless the one volunteering advice is an authorized investment adviser. Even then, unless the conversation covers only life assurance or unit trusts, yet another offence may be committed – that of 'an unsolicited verbal communication'. By no stretch of imagination could such an exchange of views be regarded as unethical but it would be illegal, however ridiculous this may appear.

Another example where prescriptive regulation goes well beyond what commonsense would hold to be a prohibition of unethical behaviour is in the Takeover Panel's ban on advertising by parties to a contested takeover. Obviously such advertising could be unethical in individual cases but it is by no means obvious that this will necessarily be so in all cases. A waste of money, possibly even foolishly counter-productive, but immoral, no.

The firmest basis for determining what is or is not ethical in financial operations would seem to rest in the common law concept of fiduciary duty. This covers the conduct of agents *vis-à-vis* their principals or clients, of trustees *vis-à-vis* beneficiaries and of directors *vis-à-vis* the shareholders of their companies; it governs the essential areas of conflict of interest, best advice and best execution. The problem is that as a principle of common law it is subject to continuous re-examination and re-interpretation in the light of individual cases. Like an elephant it is easy to recognize but hard to describe to a person who has never seen the beast.

The Securities and Investments Board regulations supposedly use the same basis, and it has been claimed that they are no more than an attempt to codify and explain the principles of the common law. This of course is precisely where the difficulty lies. The process of codification has led to the construction of an ever-growing corpus of prescriptive prohibition to block abuses that may never have occurred and to ban practices which 99 times out of 100 are quite innocent in purpose and effect. The idle conversation on the golf course is just such a case.

What then is the role of financial public relations advisers in this new regulatory environment? First and most obviously they have a duty to be fully informed of the laws, regulations and codes of conduct which affect their employers or clients and to be prepared as necessary to advise on their application. In principle this role of the financial public relations specialist in his area is no different from that of specialist advisers on employment, environmental or pollution issues in their fields. Both require detailed knowledge of the relevant regulations and of the principles underlying them. In the financial field the public relations adviser's role may be subsidiary to those of the legal and financial advisers.

At the same time the adviser's role has in it an element of the diplomat's function. Perhaps the most important aspect of this, even more important than representing his principal to the outside world, is to represent the outside world to his principal. An essential aspect of this task is to monitor and report back on opinion as it develops and to endeavour to evaluate and anticipate public reaction, whether publicly expressed or not. In this the public relations adviser should play a wider part and can exercise a broader perception than the lawyer or the financial adviser. He must also be ready to stand up for what he knows to be right and be prepared to deliver an unpopular message, not neces-sarily the one the client wants to hear. This is a role which the external consultancy may be better fitted to play than the in-house executive.

When the die is cast and a line of action determined, then it is clearly the function of the financial public relations adviser, as of the advisers specializing in other fields, to ensure that the decision and the ensuing action are explained and justified in the appropriate quarters in the context in which they arise. Public relations, as opposed to product marketing, with which it has little in common, is essentially a process of achieving acceptance, or even approbation, by education in the broadest sense. The public relations adviser should remember the maxim of Virgil, one of the earliest and most successful practitioners of the art: *Felix qui potuit rerum cognoscere causas* ('Happy is he who can understand the causes of things').

Business decisions taken for good and sufficient reasons will command greater acceptance if the audiences can be led to appreciate those reasons and to understand the context within which the decisions were taken. This leaves the problem that arises if the reasons are not good or are patently insufficient. If this results in a breach of the law or of regulations made under the law or an extra-statutory code, the defence is likely under the new regime to be conducted in the courts or an administrative tribunal rather than at the bar of public opinion. It follows that the public relations adviser is likely in such an event to play a role subsidiary to the lawyers' and it will be they who formulate the response.

To sum up, the events of the last few years have led to the financial services industry, of which the City forms an important part, but only a part nonetheless, receiving greater public scrutiny in the media and in political circles than perhaps ever before. It is not evident, however, that this greater exposure has led to any much greater understanding among the general public. To achieve this remains the central task of all those engaged in financial communication.

The problem is that the immediate day-to-day interests of individual participants in the markets and their major customers may often be at variance with those of the financial community as a whole. It is, for example, by no means uncommon for companies to wish publicly to challenge rulings of the Takeover Panel. In these circumstances the collective message emerging is necessarily confused.

The current tendency to identify companies by reference to powerful individuals only adds to the confusion. In some cases this has gone so far as to obscure the fundamental principle of fiduciary responsibility and bring into question whose interest the company exists to serve. With even the representative institutions themselves, which are the natural custodians of the City's good name, jockeying for position and status under the new regulatory regime, this confusion has grown greater rather than less.

Financial public relations executives should, in theory at least, be best equipped to address the problem of communicating the City's position to the public. Their first duty, however, whether working in-house or as consultants, must necessarily be to their employers of the moment and to those employers' immediate concerns. Matters might be different were the financial public relations industry organized as a profession in a manner similar to the Law Society or the accountants, so that there was a representative governing body capable of imposing standards and articulating a common view of the professional interest. Sadly perhaps, this is not the case.

Nevertheless, it is surely incumbent on every practitioner to be aware of the need to defend the City as a whole and its standards both against its critics and those who would subvert those standards for short-term advantage. Individual practitioners should bear in mind the need to see those standards maintained when advising their clients. In particular public relations professionals must be vigilant in ensuring that their own personal conduct is above reproach. It should, for example, be standard practice that no member of an agency's staff be permitted to deal in the shares of any agency client.

8

Stock Exchange listings, mergers and acquisitions

Angus Maitland and Charles Hodson

Financial public relations and investor relations practitioners have come to regard the handling of contested takeover bids and of Stock Exchange listings as the most taxing and the most revealing of all tests of their competence and effectiveness. At no other time is the quality of investor relations as much under the microscope as when a company appeals to institutions and private investors to put their money into its future, or when it has to persuade a body of shareholders that its managers are better than those of its rivals in a contested bid. Not that investor relations are important only at these times: maintaining credible communication with brokers' analysts, financial journalists and directly with shareholders is essential to the financial well-being of the company.

Contested takeovers are almost always the enforced result of a process that begins with lacklustre financial performance, ineffective or unimaginative communication with investors, and a share price falling far below the company's potential worth to its own shareholders – or to predators. Such companies are effectively 'dead in the water' and their managements have only two unpalatable alternatives: agreeing to merger terms or waiting for the inevitable arrival of a predator – climbing aboard the nearest passing ship, or waiting for the supplies to run out and the sharks to circle closer and closer.

It follows that good day-to-day financial public relations and investor relations practice will be aimed at preventing such misfortunes and preserving a company's independence. Nevertheless, some concentration on the financial public relations aspects of contested takeover bids and new issues is necessary, since these will generally bring public relations practitioners into the highly demanding processes of openly and directly pleading the case for or against the continued independence of a company, or of presenting the merits of a company persuasively in a restricted period of time.

Both Stock Exchange listing and merger and acquisitions activity have typically moved in cycles. The reasons for fluctuations in the level of listings activity are fairly clear: the more buoyant the general level of the economy and of the stock market, the more companies have ambitious expansion plans needing recourse to equity markets for funds, and the more investors have the funds available to invest in them. Prevailing long-term interest rates will also play a part; if they are relatively high, then listings and equity issues will be more attractive and more prevalent than bond issues.

The reasons for fluctuations in the numbers and values of company mergers and acquisitions are more complex, leaving far more room for argument by economists, academics and bankers. Some attacks of 'merger mania' have coincided with periods of low Stock Exchange liquidity; finding themselves holding too much paper, institutions have gratefully accepted the cash proffered by predators. At the opposite end of the spectrum, high liquidity has frequently prompted United States institutions to back predators issuing so-called 'junk bonds' to fund their acquisitions.

On a different tack, generally low levels of company profitability may mean that, within particular sectors, poorly-managed companies suffer more than their competitors, with the resulting drop in share price making them more tempting to a predator. Conversely, high levels of company profitability may give well-managed companies such a share price advantage that they can contemplate acquisitions of companies of the same or even of a greater size.

Tables 8.1 and 8.2 chart the changing market environment for listings and mergers and acquisitions activity since 1976. The numbers of companies coming on to the Stock Exchange were increasing in the late 1970s, but a glance at the average proceeds of new listings reveals that the primary market was as sluggish as the general level of economic activity. The early 1980s saw a steady reversal of this trend. In 1981 listing proceeds soared to £2,909m (£3,890m at 1987 prices) as sixty-three companies came on to the Exchange, nearly double the number in 1980. With the recovery in the economy, and government initiatives to encourage new businesses, listings have stayed at a high level, with the average proceeds on a plateau of roughly £170m.

Mergers and acquisitions have followed a rather different and at times contrary trend in recent years, picking up in 1978 and then falling back in 1981 (see Table 8.2). However, the turn-round in the United Kingdom economy since 1982 saw a rapid surge in activity, with the total value of companies changing hands in 1986 topping £13.5bn, and the average value at a record £50m for each company in the second quarter of the year.

There the trend was to falter. The end of 1986 saw the eruption of the insider dealing scandal surrounding the Guinness bid for Distillers;

Table 8.1   Stock Exchange listings

	Average proceeds (£m)	Total UK proceeds (£m)	Companies listed	
			UK	Other
1976	70.50	1,269	18	19
1977	50.16	1,204	24	15
1978	39.89	1,396	35	08
1979	32.83	1,608	49	13
1980	47.06	1,647	35	28
1981	46.17	2,909	63	28
1982	52.88	3,120	59	21
1983	57.99	4,581	79	36
1984	103.46	9,001	87	84
1985	173.07	13,846	80	18
1986	170.96	23,250	136	33
1987	171.98	26,657	155	34

Source: Stock Exchange

Table 8.2   Mergers and acquisitions activity

Year	Companies acquired	Total expenditure (£m)	Average expenditure (£m)
1976	353	448	1.27
1977	481	824	1.71
1978	567	1,140	2.01
1979	534	1,656	3.10
1980	469	1,475	3.14
1981	452	1,144	2.53
1982	463	2,206	4.76
1983	447	2,344	5.24
1984	568	5,475	9.64
1985	474	7,090	14.96
1986: 1	108	2,092	19.37
2	128	6,379	49.84
3	207	2,831	13.68
4	252	2,232	8.86
Total	695	13,534	19.47
1987: 1	216	3,577	16.56
2	294	4,682	15.93
3	352	3,774	10.67

Source: Central Statistical Office

early in 1987 BTR withdrew its bid for Pilkington. The bout of 'merger mania' seemed to have passed. In the first ten weeks of 1987 bids worth only £1.4bn were launched, whereas in the same period of 1986 bids totalled some £7.6bn. But with the spring the raiders emerged from their bunkers to notch up some £12bn in mergers and acquisitions by the end of the third quarter. The strong – and ill-fated – bull market continued to provide the financial impetus behind a series of deals made possible by the City's willingness to accept paper.

Whether the dramatic slump in world equity markets of October 1987 will confirm a long-term downward trend in mergers and acquisitions remains to be seen. The dynamics of the capitalist system suggest otherwise.

The Guinness affair served to remind a wider public that, far from being able to conduct their own affairs as they wished, the mandarins of blue chip companies and their merchant bankers were subject not only to the City Code on Takeovers and Mergers but also to statutory norms enforceable with the full weight of criminal law, in particular the 1985 Companies Act's provisions on insider trading.

Of more direct relevance to the vast majority of companies concerned with mergers and acquisitions, however, is the legally binding framework imposed by the Office of Fair Trading and the Monopolies and Mergers Commission, and the powers invested in the Secretary of State for Trade and Industry. He or she may impose a statutory order preventing a merger if it is felt to be against the public interest in the sense that it brings about the acquisition of gross assets of £30m or more, and results in the two merged companies holding a quarter or more of the market in any one category of goods or services. The Monopolies and Mergers Commission has the task of making the necessary recommendation to the Secretary of State; the Office of Fair Trading may give guidance but not a definitive undertaking to a company anxious to know whether an acquisition it contemplates is likely to be acceptable.

Lobbying for a referral can be a devastating weapon in the armoury not only of companies defending themselves from a bid, but also of bidders anxious to defeat a rival. Financial public relations practitioners played an important role in, for example, Gruppo Ferruzzi's efforts to obtain a Monopolies and Mergers Commission referral in its battle with Tate and Lyle for British Sugar.

The City Code on Takeovers and Mergers, the code of practice issued for the Council for the Securities Industry and administered by the Takeover Panel, had been established in the late 1960s, but even in the revised form in which it was reissued in April 1985 found itself ineffective in thwarting the more aggressive corporate raiders and their advisers in their determination to win through whatever apparent obstacles the Code imposed. Although there was to be a decline at least in the scale of the takeover battles following the Guinness affair, the Panel decided to impose a ban on advertising by either party to a bid, with only a few tightly defined exceptions, notably product or corporate image advertising.

Thus strengthened, the Code continues to be the mergers and acquisitions equivalent of the Marquess of Queensberry Rules, and throughout a bid the blue plastic ring-bound volume, or Blue Book, issued and updated by the Panel, ballasts the briefcase of competing chairman, merchant banker, corporate lawyer and communication consultant alike. Its strictures do not have the force of law, although a decision by the Court of Appeal late in 1987 made clear that the Code was a legal document and its workings – and in particular the deliberations of the Panel itself – could, for example, be subjected to judicial review under certain circumstances. Nevertheless, its authority derives from the fact that the Stock Exchange expects all its members to comply with the Code and will impose severe sanctions on those quoted companies that defy it. It also has the support of the Bank of England (which appoints its chairman and deputy chairman), the Confederation of British Industry, and a number of influential City professional associations and bodies.

Communication practitioners as well as other professional advisers have fallen foul of this practice, and it is advisable to consult the Panel wherever possible before undertaking a course of action which it may interpret as being a contravention of the Code.

The Code contains rules under a number of headings. Its central principle is the equal treatment of all shareholders; most of its rules stem from this aim. It lays down how the initial approach should be made, and how the identity of the bidder must be revealed; it demands absolute confidentiality where price-sensitive information is concerned; it lays down when and in what form the offer is to be made, and under what circumstances it may be withdrawn; it obliges directors to act in shareholders' interests and not their own; it dictates the time limit within which an offer document must be posted to the target company's shareholders and what points the document must cover; it upholds a high quality of truthfulness in all statements made by either party to a bid, and prevents them from making misleading statements; it forbids the creation of a false market in the shares of any company involved in a bid; it gives sufficient time for both parties to set out their positions and for shareholders to consider a bid; and it sets out a strict timetable for the progress of the bid.

Of overriding concern to the financial communication adviser is Rule 19 of the Takeover Code, which should be studied carefully. It covers the supply of information during a bid and contains four distinct clauses.

Clause 19.1 states that 'information about companies involved in a takeover must be made equally available to shareholders as nearly as possible at the same time and in the same manner'. Clause 19.2 contains the restrictions on advertising referred to above. Clause 19.3 dictates that any documents or announcements or anything released to the press must be lodged with the Panel and distributed to the advisers to all other parties. Clause 19.4 states that everything including details of shareholders provided to a 'preferred offeror' must equally be given to 'a less welcome but bona fide offeror or potential offeror'.

A series of notes to Rule 19 amplify it considerably and make clear the extent to which financial public relations activity is constrained during a bid.

The ban on advertising is qualified by a note exempting product or corporate advertising, non-controversial factual information, financial results or anything required or permitted by the Stock Exchange or the Panel itself. However, in an advertisement 'the making of a misleading statement is a serious matter' which a subsequent correction cannot put right. Advertisements therefore have to include a statement of responsibility by the directors. Although the Panel does clear certain advertisements if given 24 hours to do so, its clearance does not mean that it has verified the factual information they contain. The notes also warn that meetings of selected shareholders of any party to a bid may find directors giving their views on the takeover. The Code therefore insists that such meetings may not be held until after an offer document has been published and the target company's board has given its views; all shareholders have to be invited, and so do financial journalists and news agencies; and any new information that emerges has to be passed on to shareholders in a posted circular. If the information cannot be substantiated according to the demands of other parts of the Code, the circular has to withdraw it formally.

The same applies to television or radio discussions. The Panel makes it quite clear that it frowns on these, warning directors of companies engaged in a bid that they may be drawn into revealing fresh information, with the consequences described above. It also takes a particularly strong stand against any broadcast confrontation between rivals in a bid, which it feels may lead to 'gladiatorial combat'.

More specifically, directors and officials are also warned to be very careful about what they say to the press, particularly on such matters as future profits and prospects, asset values and any possibility of a revised offer. Furthermore, what has already been said in the press (or, according to a recent Panel decision, by analysts in published circulars) cannot be quoted later by parties to a bid, unless it can be substantiated and given the imprimatur of the customary directors' responsibility statement.

Organized telephone campaigns, although virtually unknown in the UK, are not prohibited by the Code. However, shareholders or groups of shareholders may be approached by telephone with the Panel's permission, provided the callers are given a script which conforms to the Code, and have a responsible financial adviser present throughout.

The notes to Rule 19 conclude by stating that financial advisers rather than communication advisers are responsible to the Panel for ensuring that information released to the media during the bid conform to the Code – an important illustration of how crucial it can be for financial public relations practitioners to enjoy good relations with other professionals advising a client.

In addition, all parties to a bid and their advisers have to bear in mind the obligatory timetable for contested takeovers (see Table 8.3).

Table 8.3   The Takeover Code's timetable for contested bids

D − 28
Announcement of firm intention to bid.
Bidder is bound to proceed with offer.
Bidder has 28 days to issue formal offer document.

D Day
Posting of the offer document.
Remainder of timetable is based on this day.

D + 14
Board of defending company to advise its shareholders of its views on the offer through the posting of the formal defence document.

D + 21
First closing date of the offer.
Further closing dates to be specified.
When offer goes unconditional, 14 days' notice in writing must be given before the offer is closed.

D + 39
Last date for the defending company to publish new information to bolster its case, e.g. announcement of results, profit or dividend forecasts, asset valuations or dividend payments.

D + 42
All conditions to be fulfilled or the offer must lapse. 21 days from the first closing date or date when offer becomes unconditional.

D + 60
Last day for declaration of an offer being made unconditional (midnight).

Clearly, such a complex set of rules provides the communication adviser with a whole series of problems. In struggling to be fair to both sides during the progress of a bid, the Code actually has the effect of favouring the predator. The target company does not know when or even if a bid is about to be launched; it cannot carry out a full programme of research about its rival; and its communication strategy has to be planned and implemented within a very narrow space of time. The only possible advantage it can hope for is an in-built bias in favour of an incumbent management on the part of its shareholders, although this will depend very much on whether it has communicated effectively with them in the past. However, a predator too will benefit from having an existing investor relations strategy.

The Code does not impose so tight a straitjacket that the communication adviser cannot vastly improve his client's chances of success by imaginative and determined financial public relations. The Code would be an absurdity if its effect were to prevent meaningful communication with shareholders at the very time that they have to make the most critical decisions about the future of their investments. The aim of Rule 19 is to prevent takeover battles from degenerating into shouting matches in which rival parties trade insults and half-truths, or 'beauty contests' in which skilled media performance counts for more than underlying financial data and sober consideration of the issues at stake. It can be criticized for stifling public debate, for example by discouraging live television discussions of takeovers, but that is because it wants shareholders to be presented with hard facts and to be given the time to make their minds up without unnecessary distraction.

Following the suggestions outlined later on programmes for takeover bids and defences, and Stock Exchange listings, communication advisers can play a powerful role in helping their client get over a message which stays within the bounds of the Code but which provides a cogent platform of support for their client's case.

Companies coming on to the Stock Exchange for the first time are vetted carefully in the interests of investors. The Stock Exchange's regulations for listing are commonly known as the Yellow Book after the yellow plastic ring binder (similar to the blue one used for the Takeover Code) which contains them, and are issued under a Statutory Instrument, the Stock Exchange Listings Regulations 1984 (itself in turn issued in implementation of three European Community directives), and the Financial Services Act 1986. Most of the Yellow Book's requirements on the provision of listing particulars therefore have full statutory force.

New listings of securities fall under several headings: ordinary voting shares, preference shares, debt securities, convertible debt securities, guaranteed issues of debt securities (where, say, a quoted holding company guarantees a debt issue by one of its subsidiaries). However, let us concentrate only on the financial public relations issues applying to companies floating their shares on the London Stock Exchange for the first time, although other listings will need similar but probably less extensive communication programmes to ensure success.

Smaller companies seeking a quotation on the Unlisted Securities Market have to fulfil broadly similar but rather less extensive requirements than those seeking a full listing. Again, the general communication principles are similar but are not specifically covered here, as the USM attracts far less media attention than the Stock Exchange, and is followed by a far smaller number of analysts. (Larger broking houses may have about four analysts assigned to the entire USM, as against forty or fifty covering the main Exchange.)

New listings can also take several forms, of which three predominate. *Offers for sale* generally receive most publicity, as they make the shares generally available to the public at a fixed, underwritten price. A quoted company, normally a bank, sponsors its client's admission to the Exchange. All the UK government's major privatizations have followed this pattern.

With *placings*, the sponsor offers the shares to its private and institutional clients, with at least a quarter going to brokers so that they can be offered to the public.

Foreign firms coming on to the London Exchange but quoted on other stock exchanges usually go for what is known as *an introduction*, which does not call for any new share issue.

New listings entail the submission to the Stock Exchange of a very large number of documents: long and short form accountants' reports, indebtedness comfort letters, specimen share certificates, and many others. However, from the financial public relations point of view, the key requirement of the Yellow Book is the preparation of a document known as the Listing Particulars, which has to contain a long series of basic items of information. In addition, the Committee on Quotations of the Stock Exchange may require companies to supply additional information on demand.

The Listing Particulars document contains a comprehensive range of information about the issuers, their financial advisers and auditors and the people responsible for the accuracy of the particulars; details of the securities to be listed; and the company's business and its financial performance. But the document must not be a salesman's pitch. The 1958 Prevention of Fraud (Investments) Act prohibits companies from pushing their shares. The Listing Particulars, detailed as they are, simply demonstrate that the company has a good record without directly attempting to lever the reader into applying for shares.

The Stock Exchange does not impose as extensive a timetable on listings as the Takeover Panel does on mergers and acquisitions. In practical terms companies generally work to a three- to four-month timetable, much of it taken up with the drafting of the listing particulars and other documents, and the finalizing of their design. However, near-final drafts of all the documentation must be submitted to the Quotations Department of the Stock Exchange at least fourteen days before the day they are generally published, known as impact day. Once approved by the company's board, the final versions of all documents must be submitted two days before impact day. The price of the shares is also usually decided during this final week.

The day before impact day, the formal notice of the listing is published, in the form of an advertisement containing the listing particulars in at least one national newspaper, with a second advertisement in another giving only a formal notice. On impact day itself, the placing or under-writing agreement is signed, and information about the issue is released to the market. Once the listing has been officially granted, dealings in the new share go ahead the following day.

The central elements in any communication programme remain the same, whether they are intended to support a listing, a takeover bid or a takeover defence. Firstly, the target audience must be identified in some detail.

In Britain, this will typically divide into four closely related groups:

1 *Investing institutions* such as pension funds, unit trusts, investment trusts, insurance companies, and fund management groups (those where institutions or individuals place their funds in the hands of managers who are responsible for selecting equity investments and retain the shareholder's discretionary powers). Together these account for at least two-thirds of all funds invested in the UK, making them almost always the ultimate deciders of the success or failure of listings or contested takeovers. They tend more and more to have their own in-house buy-side analysts, adding to the already considerable sophistication they show in their investment decisions.

2 *Private individuals,* accounting for the remaining one-third of funds invested in the UK. These are rather more difficult to reach, although the series of major UK government privatization issues have shown the value of using such devices as national television and press advertising linked with free telephone calls for those wishing to be sent prospectuses. In takeover battles individual shareholders receive offer documents, defence documents and any

subsequent chairmen's letters through the post, but (to the extent that they read such documents in any detail) are liable to recognize their necessarily partisan nature and may discount them. Almost certainly, the best way to influence individual shareholders is to approach them through the two remaining segments of the target audience.

3   *Brokers' analysts* (increasingly known as sell-side analysts to distinguish them from the major institutions' in-house buy-side analysts), whose circulars provide institutions, financial advisers and, to a much lesser extent, individual shareholders with intelligence about the outlook for industry sectors as well as individual shares. Each broker or securities house usually subdivides its research department into groups, each containing between two and six analysts assigned to cover a particular industry sector. Financial public relations practitioners will need to identify the single analyst responsible for following their client, and to determine the relative weight he or she will be given by shareholders. The standard of brokers' research and of individual analysts' abilities is carefully monitored and taken into account by key investors, and organizations such as Consensus Research, Extel and *Institutional Investor* magazine actually publish research findings stating who are believed by company finance directors or institutional investors to be the top analysts in each sector.

For a listing, the backing of a majority of the most influential brokers in the form of a circular encouraging their clients to buy, is crucial to success. During a contested takeover, however, analysts tend to be extremely cautious, given the way that the situation can change rapidly. Analysts are always reluctant to alienate either side unless the outcome is crystal clear. Telephone briefings rather than written circulars are the normal way of providing their clients with a running commentary on developments such as revised offers.

4   *The financial press* provides a powerful vehicle for reaching individual shareholders, institutions and sell-side analysts alike. All three groups are painfully aware that, however satisfied they may be with what they think goes on in the equity marketplace, it *is* a marketplace, and what will predominate will not be fundamentals (objectively definable factors such as past company performance) so much as the view of the majority, even though that view may at times be badly mistaken. Thus the financial press is keenly read as a regularly updated pointer to what other participants in the market are likely to think and do.

Again the financial public relations practitioner will need to identify those journalists likely to be writing about his or her client, and to ensure that interest is maintained by speaking to business news editors and columnists on a regular basis.

Secondly, it is vital to find out what the target audience thinks about a company. Here, it is often surprising to realize the extent to which a supposedly well briefed and perceptive group of people can be swayed by prejudice, or may entertain quite eccentric but nonetheless strongly held views on the basis of very little knowledge. This is particularly true of companies which are moving on to the Stock Exchange for the first time, or which have attracted little attention from analysts, journalists or institutions. With a listing, the process of finding out what the target audience thinks can be much easier, because time is on the company's side, and the timing of the listing can be chosen rather than imposed.

Here, a programme of research conducted by a reputable market research company can be of enormous assistance in identifying those misconceptions which need to be addressed as the listing communication campaign gets under way. The format and wording of the questionnaire have to be carefully chosen, as do the respondents. Those working in the financial sector are busy people, and a number of them are likely to be irritated, if not alienated, by ham-fisted interviewing by inexperienced researchers asking ill-considered questions. Like everyone else, analysts and fund managers dislike being asked about things they realize they do not know about, so questions apparently designed to chart their ignorance should be avoided.

In the case of takeovers, time is far more pressing. The Blue Book discourages direct contact with shareholders, whether institutions or individuals, on the grounds that this violates the principle of equal treatment of shareholders. In any case, once a bid is announced, it may be some time before the financial public relations consultancy advising the would-be victim has access to a full copy of the share register. As for journalists, unless the bid is for a well known and frequently covered company, they are likely to be relatively uninformed. The immediate step therefore is to get in touch with analysts by telephone, and to identify and gauge the views of those likely to be following the bid. In terms of formal research an attitude survey among the defending company's shareholders can provide crucial information on which to base an effective communication programme. The Panel insists the sponsor of the research is made known to all interviewees.

The third step is to work out the unique selling proposition (to borrow a piece of consumer marketing jargon) which is to form the backbone of the communication programme. What can your clients do better than anyone else? What makes their products special? What makes their management so special? Why should investors put their financial faith in them? What gives them the right to think they can run the takeover victim better than the existing management, or offer the victim's shareholders a better deal by cashing in their shares or exchanging them for shares in a company of which they may know very little? What makes them so sure they ought to remain independent?

Coming from outside and seeing the company through the eyes of an outsider, the communication consultant often has a huge advantage in identifying his client's strong and weak points, although he or she may face a problem in later persuading the client to see things in the same way.

The message that emerges has to be distinctive and memorable, and it has to be seen to be relevant by the target group. Moreover, it has to be reiterated at every possible opportunity, using every device available: formal documents, results literature, press or analyst briefings, institutional presentations, meetings with shareholders, site visits, press comment and broadcast interviews.

Video provides a short cut to providing the target audience with a clear and dynamic picture of what the company does, what its products are and who buys them, who its managers are and what their strengths are, and of how it is likely to develop. But video has to be well produced and of obvious relevance. Television is seen by many serious-minded observers as an entertainment medium which does not fit in with the business of assessing financial prospects. Some even dismiss it as mere gimmickry, while press and radio journalists can have a jaundiced view of the influence wielded by their television counterparts. But these are minority views and carefully prepared video has played a useful part in communication campaigns of all types, even in takeover battles (although here the Takeover Panel has to vet all videos before they can be shown to investors).

It is important not to follow set formulae. It is easy to forget that fund managers, analysts and journalists spend their working lives being bombarded with the efforts of financial public relations practitioners to focus their attention on their clients. For them, one company can look very much like another and they can become blasé. The managements that can survive and prosper without being distinctive in their communications are very few.

A crucial building block in the success of financial public relations is a strong relationship not only with the client company but also with its financial advisers. In listings and takeovers alike the merchant or investment bank must necessarily play the lead role among the advisers. The more confidence, trust and respect clients, merchant bankers and communication consultants have for each other, the more likely it is that they can achieve their objectives. Within this relationship each party must know its role, and avoid straying into each other's territory.

Throughout a communication campaign, the work of public and investor relations consultants coincides with that of other professionals: lawyers must check press releases during takeover campaigns, accountants need to verify financial information, and so on.

Effective partnerships between merchant banks and communication consultants often continue with different clients. Merchant banks not infrequently recommend particular communication consultancies or individuals to their clients on the basis of the success they have enjoyed together in advising quite different clients.

Media training can also be a useful adjunct to a communication campaign. Even the best communicators in the boardroom can find themselves at a loss when dealing with an unexpected question from a journalist, and television or even radio can be cruel media to those unfamiliar with the way they work. It is important that those likely to come into contact with the media take the time to spend half a day practising their skills with journalists who subject them to mock interviews.

The most important point of all is that communication campaigns are never marginal or merely cosmetic, particularly not at times of listings, mergers or acquisitions. The public and investor relations adviser is not a 'bolt-on goodie' working purely to enhance the outward appearance of the company. His or her work is a crucial component in the company's efforts to raise investor support, and he or she should enjoy the same kind of access to the chairman, finance director and other senior directors as any other member of the advisory team.

The best time to fight off a predator is before he has even had time to think of launching his attack. The best time to secure an acquisition is before it has even been identified. Here professional communication advisers can play a large part in developing a reservoir of understanding of the company among its shareholders. To borrow an analogy from military strategy, such a communication programme allows for defence in depth in the event of a takeover or merger initiative. A predator will have to work hard throughout the takeover battle to reverse the momentum of goodwill built up by an effective investor relations programme.

Although this topic is approached more or less from the victim's point of view, would-be predators will find that communicating not only with their own shareholders but also with a broader audience of investors, analysts and journalists will make their task far easier when it comes to winning over their victim's shareholders and persuading them to accept an offer.

A number of factors may lead to short-term financial performance difficulties. Profits may be badly affected by any of a number of unforeseen or unavoidable factors, such as political changes in an overseas market, currency fluctuations, a strike in a supplier or client company, and restructuring or redundancy costs. When things go wrong, it is essential not only for managements to explain to investors why performance has been affected and when profits are likely to recover, but also to have in place the kind of long-nurtured relationship with analysts and journalists that allows them to communicate from a platform of credibility and consistency.

Some companies let the best chances to better their relationship with key investors pass them by. Annual and interim results should be treated as heaven-sent opportunities to invite financial journalists, fund managers and analysts to meet senior directors, whether at a formal press conference, informal briefings or lunches, or at a combination of all three. This allows for good results to receive the widest possible currency, and for poor ones to be put into their proper context. Such meetings also provide companies with a platform from which to discuss their future plans and the outlook for their operations, and to correct any misconceptions about past performance or future prospects.

The annual general meeting is another useful time at which to cement shareholder loyalty by providing an informative and inviting forum for individual investors as well as brokers and institutions to meet management.

Following on from annual results, annual reports provide an excellent opportunity for companies to place their achievements on record. The annual report is treated as an essential for desk research by analysts, fund managers and journalists alike, and should be treated as a showpiece of the company's ability not only to produce impressive financial results but also to present itself in an arresting and informative way. Too many annual reports are treated as a necessity, with few concessions to readability or visual attractiveness. Some even fail to tell the casual reader what goods or services the company actually provides, or even what business it is in. These are obvious turn-offs for individual investors, who usually have to read such documents in their own time and whose support may well prove critical to the outcome of an eventual bid. As for analysts and fund managers, they always insist that they look at the figures in black and white, but the reality is that they, like everyone else deluged with paper on a daily basis, are likely to pay more attention to a good-looking annual report than one which presents only a bland, boring, backward-looking image of a company.

The annual report should be available not just to existing share-holders but to those investors, particularly institutions, who do not yet own shares in the company but might be expected to do so. Besides fulfilling a central role in the development of a compelling annual report, the communication consultant should also advise on obtaining the widest possible circulation of the final product among potential new shareholders.

Corporate advertising can provide another useful way of presenting an attractive image for a company when its share price may be in the doldrums. This may be particularly appropriate where there is a 'performance gap', for example, between the identification of a problem, remedial management action and an eventual lift in the share rating. The advertising should aim to generate a good image specifically for the company's management, with sell-side analysts and institutions as its main target groups.

It goes without saying that slack management will attract predators. Failure to deal with pressing problems within the company, such as a subsidiary which consistently makes losses or which is perceived by key investors and observers not to fit, is a blatant invitation to a predator and a severe disadvantage for a company wishing to prove that it can offer better leadership than a takeover target's existing management.

Credible, regular communication with analysts and journalists will provide at the very least an insurance policy against failure to get the company's message over during the tense days of a takeover battle, when chairmen and senior directors are likely to find themselves stuck behind the scenes attending to essential financial business. It may boil down simply to knowing key analysts and journalists on first name terms – a state of affairs which can later allow far more progress to be made in the short time available during a bid. Moreover, those chairmen who enjoy a relaxed and confident relationship with journalists and, in particular, analysts are far more likely to be told what their company's blemishes are in the eyes of the City, and thus to be given the chance to take action in good time.

Computerized analysis of the shareholder register has not yet developed in the UK to quite the extent that it has in the US, where the trading and regulatory systems have allowed stock surveillance to catch on among many companies, and not just the larger ones. By searching out the identities behind nominee names and by analyzing the changes in the shareholder register, companies are given ample warning of stake-building by would-be predators, and are able to identify their most significant shareholders when it comes to targetting investor relations programmes.

Predators have the huge advantages of being able to prepare their takeover strategy before the bid is launched, can control the timing and have the element of surprise working for them. To make the best use of these, they should bring together the key members of their team of advisers as early as possible, so that thorough research can be undertaken, and they can make major decisions about how the bid is to be presented to the City and to the target company's shareholders.

It is useful at this point to run through the entire bid timetable (see Table 8.3) trying to forecast how events will turn out, who will need to be contacted when, what briefings and visits are to take place, and – most critically – what arguments the defenders are likely to deploy. Those bidders who fail to put their own houses in order and find themselves unable to answer criticisms voiced by their would-be victims can pay a heavy price, and possibly even face a hostile takeover attempt themselves.

If well defended, the would-be victim may launch its counter-attack on any of a number of areas, and the pre-offer period is a good time for professional advisers to think of areas in which their client may be vulnerable. How strong is the company's own financial record? Are questions likely to be raised about its record on dividend payments, earnings per share, or the value of shareholders' funds? How good is its record when it comes to handling acquisitions? Have those who held shares in its previous victims and who sold out for shares been satisfied that they made the right decision? Is the quality of the company's management likely to be called into question? The sooner questions like these can be considered, the more effectively the communication consultant can work out how to answer them or even to pre-empt them.

A would-be predator should cling to the advantage he enjoys from being allowed to launch an attack at a time of his own choosing. It is important to dictate the terms on which the takeover battle will be fought, usually by putting forward an unstoppable unique selling proposition on the day the bid is announced. Industrial synergy, the weakness of the incumbent management, improved cash flow: these are just some of the arguments which predators have managed to put over to analysts and financial journalists in such a way that the defending management never succeeds in bringing to the fore the arguments it believes will support its case.

Not that the first day of the bid is the most important: the ten days running up to closing dates are the most important. Few shareholders make up their minds whether to accept offers until the last minute, for the obvious reason that they first want to see how the two companies' share prices compare. So communication effort needs to be concentrated on this period above all.

As ever, the major investing institutions will probably decide the outcome of the bid. Some of their fund managers and buy-side analysts will be familiar with the bidding company, but some of those institutions who appear on the defender's shareholder register (which the Blue Book obliges him to divulge to the bidder) may need to be courted with background briefings and site visits in addition to those laid on for all fund managers, analysts and journalists.

One of the ways in which the Takeover Code favours the predator derives from an important exception to its blanket ban on advertising:

'. . . advertisements which are product or corporate image advertisements not bearing on an offer or potential offer'. In practice this means that a corporate advertising campaign which is already well under way when a bid is announced can continue. Clearly, a bidder can benefit enormously from his advantage of surprise here by making up an advertisement and booking media space in the full knowledge that its main purpose will be to support his takeover attempt.

The disadvantage is that seasoned City observers, who are familiar with this gambit, may well see such a corporate advertising campaign as a fairly unmistakable hint that a bid is imminent, and will then start speculating about who might be its victim. This in turn will make stake-building more expensive, possibly prohibitively so.

The choice of a communication consultant able to carry out the kind of programme needed can be difficult. It is best to avoid the kind of financial public relations practitioner known for his or her ability, on a Friday evening, to give spurious tips to the Sunday newspapers; such consultancies do not have the credibility which may be needed when it comes to putting over the key arguments to observers during the bid. It is also important, if a significant part of the communication work is to be prepared or conducted before the bid is announced, to ensure that total confidentiality can be maintained.

Good management and sound financial performance, even if combined, are not a 100 per cent effective 'shark repellent', and may even attract raiders. The motives of rationalization, improving market share, bringing high quality executives on to the payroll, or simply gaining assets which might prove expensive to buy on the open market are all factors that may prompt a predator to pay well over the odds for a competitor company. Moreover, these are enemies that can prove hard to fight in the breathless timetable within which a takeover defence must be mounted.

Despite the pressure of time, the outline programme set out earlier should be followed. It may not be possible to carry out all its stages as fully as in a listing programme, but there are ways of abbreviating them. For example, on the day the bid is announced the communication consultancy can ring all the analysts that cover the sector to find out their views on the bid and to alert them to the fact that a stout defence campaign will be mounted. City news-desks can be contacted to find out which journalists will be following the bid, and to offer immediate reaction from the defending management's spokesmen, and so on. This is scarcely as satisfactory as a full-scale programme which is intelligently prepared and well researched, but it will nevertheless play a central role in the success or failure of the defence.

Just as the bidding company should try to hold on to the communication initiative and should try to dictate the terms of the debate throughout the takeover battle, the defending management should try even harder to win it back. Often it may not be the weight of the arguments that are put up that matters as much as whether or not they are put over in an effective and timely manner. Once a powerful argument has come to dominate the debate, it becomes difficult to dislodge.

Defending chairmen or chief executive officers sometimes tend to become mesmerized by the iron timetable, the busy round of meetings with the financial advisers, the need to put out lengthy documents containing a lot of detailed and carefully verified information, and the stress of worrying about whether they will have a job in a few weeks' time. Like all the other advisers, the communication consultant is there to lighten all these burdens by offering the reassurance of his extensive experience of takeovers. In return the top person must make doubly sure that the best use is made of his or her time, and that time and thought are spent on how the company's message should best be presented.

The defending management should take advantage of its right to inject additional information on its future financial performance into the debate. The early announcement of financial results, revaluations of asset values or dividend payments and above all the publishing of profit and dividend forecasts must be used wherever possible to take full advantage of the opportunities offered by the Code. (A successful defence against a takeover bid is described in Case Study 2, page 156.)

The most successful pre-listing communication programmes begin many months before impact day. Those for major offers for sale – for example, for government privatization issues – usually start a year or more before, with heightened general public relations designed to raise awareness among employees as well as to obtain a higher external profile for the company. If commercial considerations allow, this is advisable in all cases, as is a warning to the press and to analysts that a listing can be expected.

In addition, a programme of corporate advertising provides a powerful springboard if initiated roughly six months before impact day. Such campaigns should stress not only the desirability of the company's products but also its commercial success and possibly even the strengths of its management. If a unique selling proposition has been developed, then this can be alluded to, but without wearing it out before it can be properly developed and presented with maximum public impact during the listing programme itself.

The specific programme should start five months before impact day with a research study aimed at identifying the City view of the company. This highlights the problems the company may encounter when it appeals for funds, and provides the basis of the communication strategy for the next four months. This is the stage at which a general meeting between the company and all members of its advisory team should be held, providing everyone concerned with the listing with a chance to hear how and when the listing is to be approached, to establish what their responsibilities will be, and to meet one another and gain a feel for the way the relationship between the teams of advisers will be cemented over the coming weeks. A general tour of as many of the company's sites as possible will be invaluable at this stage; it gives the communication team a chance to work out which sites will be of most interest to journalists when the time comes to invite them to see the company's operations for themselves.

With the date of impact day now finalized, an early decision in principle about which media of communication are to be used should be made. It will help greatly with planning advertising, design and print production work, and video production.

Four months before impact day, the general outlines of the communication programme should already be apparent, and the unique selling proposition clearly identified and understood by all parties. The design of the prospectus and listing particulars and of all supporting material now becomes an important priority, with the communication consultancy's creative and design team being briefed on what documents they will be expected to work on, and how they should look. Prospectus advertising should be planned and media space booked.

Another priority will be the design, approval and production of supporting material, particularly the contents of basic information packs to be handed out to journalists and analysts as the programme starts to unfold. If the company has a corporate brochure, it should be updated and if necessary redesigned.

This is also the point at which preparations for any video should be taken a step further, with the establishment of shooting schedules and the preparation of an outline script.

A month later, supporting material should start to emerge from the production pipeline, and the information packs can be assembled and distributed. Meanwhile, corporate advertising and prospectus advertising concepts and designs should be submitted for approval, and the space for them booked in newspapers and, if selected, with television companies.

Dates are set for separate meetings with selected journalists, analysts and fund managers. These can be followed immediately afterwards by less formal lunches, with invitation lists drawn up by the financial public relations team. These provide an informal atmosphere in which key analysts and journalists can get to know the company's chairman and senior directors and expand their own understanding of the company.

The dates for general press conferences and analyst and institutional investor meetings in the immediate run-up to impact day can also be finalized and the venues booked.

Three months before impact day, the listings particulars should be going into their second or third draft, with their design outlines already clear, and two months before impact day the first proofs should be available. The communication campaign enters into full swing, with the company's message already being put forward at the first of a series of one-to-one lunches with key investors, such as the fund managers of those blue chip institutions thought to be interested in subscribing to the new issue.

Later that month the prospectus appears, and an initial campaign of press advertising is used to appeal to individual shareholders to apply for copies of the prospectus and share application form. The video should now be available and approved, ready to be shown to journalists, analysts and fund managers.

In the final six weeks before impact day, the programme of contacts is moving faster and the preparation of documents is moving into its final stages, leaving more time for senior directors to spend on the communication programme. The consultancy is by now monitoring the press carefully to identify new issues and problems as they emerge, and to refine the process of inviting journalists to site visits and private briefings.

Presentations are made to investing institutions, with plenty of time allotted to question and answer sessions. These should always be preceded if possible by rehearsals at which the communication consultancy uses its understanding of the way the target audience is thinking to give the chairman and senior directors the chance to practise their answers to possible questions.

Several larger companies have benefited from the use of launch events to heighten still further awareness of their imminent listing. Before Big Bang the hexagonal booths on the Stock Exchange floor could be used for display material such as large replica telephones at the time of the British Telecom privatization, and model unicorns (the corporate symbol of the Wellcome Foundation) when Wellcome was listed in the largest-ever flotation of a private company on the London market (see Case Study 1, p.151). Since Big Bang, even larger stages are used: a fly-past for Rolls-Royce, and holograms and a low-flying Concorde over the Thames for British Airways.

Through the medium of television, such events naturally attract wide public interest, but they also add a feeling among institutions that a stock will be scarce because of demand from individual investors. They can of course be overdone; it is questionable whether they will be sustainable in terms of public interest in the post-crash atmosphere.

As impact day approaches, and the deadline for share applications passes, rehearsals are held for the final press conferences, and times for broadcast interviews are fixed with television and radio news editors. Bulk prints of the listing particulars are obtained and distributed, and final queries from journalists cleared up.

The success or failure of the marketing and communication campaign – and the wisdom of the key decision on price – will become apparent as soon as it is known whether the issue is oversubscribed or undersubscribed, and becomes even more apparent once the shares start trading. But no matter how successful the listing has been, the interest should not be allowed to die down. The company must follow through with a comprehensive campaign of investor relations, capitalizing on the goodwill and understanding generated over the past few weeks.

Within the next few years financial markets and company law in the twelve member countries of the European Community will be transformed. The fifteen years since Britain's entry into the Community have already seen the pattern of trade shift radically towards mainland Europe, with a dramatic realignment of economic activity from the west coast to the east coast. If the completion of the internal market planned for 1992 goes ahead, then the impact on the pattern of company ownership and on the future development of European stock markets will be every bit as far-reaching as the impact of the gradual lowering of tariff barriers throughout Western Europe.

The late 1980s have already seen some far-sighted companies implementing a long-term strategy in which the considerations of 1992 are obvious. Anticipating the free market in financial services, the French group Compagnie du Midi bid £460m for the British financial services group Equity and Law, while the remarkable struggle by Carlo de Benedetti to take over the Belgian bank-cum-industrial conglomerate Société Generale demonstrated the need for some coherent, equitable system of conducting such battles in certain countries not accustomed to them.

British companies have been slow to capitalize on the possibilities of looking for acquisitions in Europe, apparently preferring to see more European companies take over British ones than the opposite process. The US has traditionally been the happy hunting ground of the acquisition-hungry. The common language, the relative similarity of what regulation there is, the ease of doing business, and above all the vast single market have been the basis on which empires like Hanson have been built. By contrast, a number of European countries, including France, have the kind of corporate statutory framework that either bans outright a hostile takeover attempt by a foreign company or makes it too complex for many potential predators' managements to consider.

At the same time, there is some concern about the pattern of trans-national acquisitions by those companies able to circumvent the obstacles placed in their way by national legislation. As the internal market becomes more effective, a number of the larger conglomerates find themselves exercising a growing degree of monopoly power. Given the European Community Commission's duties to uphold competition as well as the removal of barriers to free trade, action is under way at a Community level to extend the Commission's existing powers. This will prove a difficult task: national governments will not readily allow their own competition enforcement bodies to be circumvented, and there may be political complications where, for example, a gov-ernment is committed to seeing a particular merger go ahead. But the pressures for a comprehensive and comprehensible anti-monopoly framework at a European level are bound to be unstoppable in the longer term.

From that should follow further pressures, this time for a European regulatory framework for hostile takeovers to replace the Blue Book and its equivalents in other Community states. Once again, there will be difficulties stemming ultimately from the differences in atmosphere and business tradition. But it remains a certainty that by the end of this century financial public and investor relations practitioners will find themselves having to communicate to investors, shareholders and journalists across at least a dozen countries and probably more; having to consider a European Community code on information flow; and having to lobby European Community bodies for a stay of execution on the grounds that a particular takeover is anti-competitive.

This will make the task of the communication consultant much more complicated. A message that may be compelling in the City of London may well be dismissed out of hand in another financial centre; lessons may have to be learned from those in consumer advertising who know full well how selling the same product in two different countries calls for two completely different marketing approaches. Research into atti-tudes among target audiences will be an important factor in building up and supplementing the understanding of the way that investors in different countries approach financial decisions. In-depth expertise and knowledge will be at a premium, and so will information on, for example, who are the most influential financial journalists and analysts in a particular centre.

Listings are bound to be just as dramatically affected. The implemen-tation of European Community directives has already played a part in the drafting of the current UK legislative framework for Stock Exchange listings. In theory, at least, a truly free internal market with no exchange controls would give a company the ability to list wherever it wanted; if size permitted, it would probably go for a listing on several exchanges simultaneously. Again, the communication consultant would have to develop varied programmes to gain the maximum impact right across Western Europe.

With a population of 320 million people, the European Community in fact has a far greater economic potential than the United States, provided it can be opened up to create the single domestic market combined with extensive natural resources to create the richest federation in the world. But even if the 1992 free market goes ahead, plus all that will follow from it, the Community will still have nine different official languages. Under such circumstances, the prospects for communicators must be bright indeed.

Takeover battles and listings are set-piece challenges for financial public relations practitioners. They take place against a market background which is constantly changing and which must be taken into account in the development of communication programmes.

Nevertheless, companies must communicate at all times; good financial performance is not enough. It must be amplified through effective and intelligent programmes which project a positive image of the company and its management. These are designed to safeguard the company against predators, and to allow it to pursue its goals with the maximum of support and understanding from its shareholders and from the financial community generally.

As a specialist form of financial public relations, investor relations concentrates on achieving these objectives through the use of a wide variety of techniques, and through applying them on a routine basis rather than waiting for a hostile bid to be announced or allowing the interest generated by a successful flotation to fade.

In the case of takeovers and listings, the techniques that can be used are tightly controlled by a combination of statutory restrictions and self-regulation by the financial community, but the effect is to limit the way in which particular techniques are used, rather than to shorten the list of ways of projecting the company's message. A number of general underlying principles point the way towards successful communication campaigns: identification of the target audience, research into their attitudes towards the company, development and application of a unique selling proposition, good co-operation with other professional advisers, and a recognition of the importance of the communication consultant within the advisory team.

However, it is important not to follow set patterns and to remember how busy and potentially jaded members of the target audiences can be. The practice of communicating often calls for a lot of uninspiring hard work, but it must also include creative thinking to keep it fresh and interesting to its audience.

Progress towards a single market for all goods and services within the European Community will inevitably be followed by the eventual establishment of Community-wide corporate legislation and regulatory frameworks to apply to both listings and takeovers. The role of the communication consultant will thereby be complicated, but is likely to remain central to the continued effectiveness of the financial system and the free market.

9

Crisis management

Michael Regester

A survey of chief executives in the United States conducted in 1985 by Stephen B. Fink, president of Lexicon Communications, found that 89 per cent believed 'a crisis in business as inevitable as death and taxes'. Only 50 per cent admitted they had a plan for managing one.

The keys to crisis management are anticipation, planning, preparation, and training. Much of the responsibility for such action rests with the executive board of directors and the company secretary, but it is the public relations function that will be called to swing into action once the fire breaks out.

When it does, effective dealing with the communication aspects of the crisis will be as crucial as the operational response to the crisis itself. Life will be made a good deal easier for the public relations executive if the board of directors has been constantly nudged into updating its crisis contingency plans. If the board is not a self-starter in this respect, the public relations executive, in his own best interests as well as those of the company, would do well to adopt the role of corporate 'nudger'.

Crises in business can take many forms. Examples include fraud, losses, insider dealing, major theft, commercial and market disasters, computer breakdown, takeovers, and government legislation.

Each day the press is filled with intricate stories of unwanted takeover bids or companies' collapsing share prices because they have been caught napping by major changes in the consumer marketplace. Remember how the Swiss watch industry failed to foresee the impact of Japanese quartz watches?

Effective management of communication during a crisis is not just about dealing with the media. Different audiences require different handling. Effective crisis management calls for pro-active communication with shareholders, the financial community, politicians, government agencies, pressure groups and all other stakeholders who have a vested interest in the success or failure of the organization.

Although each group may need to be handled in a different way, what is important is that a consistent message runs through each statement to each group. For example, a shareholder may be hearing one story from his professional adviser and another from the company in which he has invested. Part of the art of communication management is to ensure, as far as possible, that everyone 'sings from the same hymn sheet'. To achieve this goal, a coherent approach to planning for crisis is needed.

The principles applying to crisis management planning are broadly the same for virtually all forms of corporate crisis, and the methods for implementing the plan will not vary greatly. No one can anticipate every crisis that might conceivably arise, but there are a number of steps any company can take to prepare for one.

A coherent approach begins with the identification of potential crises. These include situations that may turn critical, crises that have beset the company in the past and that might recur, and crises that are known to have affected comparable companies. For example, a company with wage negotiations looming can anticipate the possibility of work stoppage and consider the potential effects of picketing, violence, fall in production and the resultant impact on sales, profits and share price.

Danger signals can be identified. Any of the following, for instance, might lead to an unwanted takeover bid:

(a) Static or falling earnings.
(b) Poor return on capital.
(c) Unhealthy dividend policy.
(d) Bad cash management.
(e) Too high gearing.
(f) Poor investment policy.
(g) Too many, difficult-to-justify rights issues.
(h) Unimaginative asset management (including well-stocked pension fund or cash mountain).
(i) Neglected communication with shareholders and the financial community in general.
(j) Major shareholder suddenly selling off shares.
(k) Upcoming tax or protectionist legislation.
(l) Business synergy with the predator (improved earnings prospects of the combined companies).
(m) Marketing synergy.
(n) Another company knocking you out as direct competition.
(o) A competitor acquiring some of your management team.
(p) A competitor acquiring extra production capacity.

Crisis, when it applies to the financial aspects of a company's business, is usually to do with ownership, even in this, now classic, example.

The president of Norwest Bank in Minneapolis was, so the story goes, carving his Thanksgiving turkey when a friend called: 'Jim, your bank is on fire'. Some hundred miles away, the bank's vice-president of corporate communication was visiting relatives and was startled to see a television report on a major fire in downtown Minneapolis.

What was to become the biggest blaze in Minneapolis' history also served as a baptism of fire for Norwest Bank's crisis contingency plans. Six months earlier the company had updated its public relations plan, the main purpose of which was to assure customers that, in the event of an emergency, their funds were safe and business would continue as usual. The revised plan provided for the location of vital back-up records, telephone numbers of key executives to be notified, and the availability of office space should departments have to be relocated at short notice.

Even as the flames gutted the 16-storey structure, the public relations plan was activated. The bank's president went on radio and television advising depositors that accounts and valuables were safe, the building fully insured and that all other branches would open for business the following day.

With a staff of a dozen bank public relations people as well as personnel from two outside firms, the bank set up special telephone hotlines for customers, employees and the media from a 'war room' established in a building across the street. The press were given unlimited access to bank executives. Personal letters were sent and phone calls made from appropriate departmental heads to allay any fears that assets were in danger. 'A lot of people are unsophisticated', observed the bank's vice-president of corporate communication. 'They think if a bank burns, their money burns with it.'

When Norwest reopened for business, bank representatives, easily identified by red and white T-shirts emblazoned 'NW Bank Info', were spotted throughout downtown Minneapolis directing customers to bank locations.

In all, the crisis programme cost Norwest about $400,000. Later, the bank's president remarked: 'The Thanksgiving Day fire was one of the most traumatic experiences of my life. But if you're going to have a catastrophe, this is the kind to have. There was no business lost, no hostile press and nobody got hurt'. Panic had been averted.

In a sense, Norwest was lucky, but the bank deserves full credit for the fact that it had a crisis contingency plan. Not only did such a plan exist, but it had been recently revised and updated. The bank also demonstrated considerable creative initiative, for example, in using some of its representatives wearing (presumably pre-prepared) T-shirts to direct customers to other bank branches.

Norwest Bank got it right. The bank's president was not frightened to appear on television and radio to reassure and advise customers;

the bank set up telephone hotlines for customers, employees and the media; and it established a 'war room' staffed by personnel whose role it was to manage the crisis.

It boils down to deeds versus declarations. If a company is seen to be well prepared and therefore well managed, it has the best possible chance of encountering a crisis with a measure of calm and emerging with a measure of success.

The need is to catalogue the areas of potential crisis which could affect the organization you represent, and to assess the risk parameters. From this starting point, it becomes easier to think through the logical series of steps that need to be taken into account in the crisis planning process. Ask such questions as:

1   How vulnerable is the organization to a takeover?
2   Would it be strong enough to survive?
3   What additional communication measures can be put in place to strengthen the organization's defences?
4   If substantial losses are foreseeable, does the organization have a clear, strategic business plan to take it through the downturn? Are key audiences aware of the plan and its significance? Is it believable?
5   Is the company tracking government/EEC legislation sufficiently far ahead to be able to take action to argue against adverse legislation or adjust itself to accommodate it? (*Parliamentary Lobbying* by Nigel Ellis, in this series, is a useful introduction to putting the business case to government.)

These and other questions should be asked regularly by the board of directors. Too often they are not and it becomes the task of the public relations function to ensure that such questions are addressed and to lobby the board to take appropriate measures.

Having identified the areas of risk, the next questions to ask are:

(a) Does the company have policies and procedures designed to minimize the chances of a risk turning into a crisis?
(b) Should it occur, do plans for dealing with every aspect of the crisis exist?
(c) Have the plans been tested to ensure they work satisfactorily?

In short, planning for crisis management may be summarized as:

- Cataloguing potential crises.
- Devising policies for their prevention.
- Formulating strategies and tactics for dealing with each potential crisis.

- Identifying who will be affected by them.
- Devising effective communication channels to those affected so as to minimize damage to the organization's reputation.
- Testing everything.

There is a need for a crisis management team with the key role of ensuring that, as far as possible, a crisis does not develop. It needs to set company-wide policies appropriate to the risks likely to be encountered. Equally important, it must ensure that the management of each part of the business is not only given the funds or other resources required to comply with the policies, but is also responsible for implementing them.

Such policies should go beyond ensuring that the organization complies merely with existing regulations. They should endeavour to anticipate 'worst case' scenarios. Although this approach may prove costly, the costs of not setting such far-reaching policies could prove catastrophic to the company's entire future.

Developing policies against agreed company criteria will help to give them shape and depth. Such criteria can be developed by answering the following questions:

1 Would the situation really affect the bottom line?
2 How realistic is the identified potential crisis?
3 Could corporate action halt or moderate the crisis?
4 Does the policy stand up to public examination?
5 Are the resources to act available?
6 Is the cost to the company acceptable?
7 Is the will to act present?
8 What would be the effect of inaction?

A positive approach to crisis management demands that the implementation of preventive policies is checked on a regular basis. Part of the crisis management team's remit should be to conduct audits to check policy implementation. For example, the crisis management team can appoint other members of management to adopt the protagonist role of an unwanted bidder, looking for tell-tale signs of weakness in the company's performance, its ability to muster professional advisers quickly and a strategy for defence. The role-playing protagonists then report areas of weakness to the main board with recommendations for strengthening them.

The crisis management team must be ready to move into action at a moment's notice. Usually it will consist of the chairman or the chief executive, finance director and perhaps a third main board director or company secretary. It will also include the head of public relations, and representatives of the company's merchant bank, public relations consultancy and legal advisers.

Members of the crisis management team need to be relieved of all their normal day-to-day duties so that they can concentrate on the problem in hand. Other directors and executives must be seen to be getting on with running the normal operations of the company.

The communication aspects of dealing with a crisis are as crucial as the operational response of the organization at risk. Looking at an unwanted takeover bid, because it is the most likely example of a financial crisis, the first item on the agenda is to define the audience.

To be able to convince the audience, it helps to have a fairly clear idea of who they are. A breakdown of the share register should be maintained on the basis of the size of the shareholding, whether it is a private, institutional or nominee holding, its geographical area and the average length in time of the shareholding. Rights under law of discovering the identity of investors behind nominee holdings should be invoked and the broking firms involved in the larger share transactions should be monitored.

A knowledge of the size of the shareholding and details of its type should give a good indication of where the voting influence lies. The geographical spread will give an idea of where regional advertising might play a role. The length of time for which shares have been held will give an indication of shareholder loyalty. If, for example, a large proportion of a company's shareholders has held shares for around five years but the share price, profits or dividend growth have fallen considerably over that same period, continued shareholder loyalty might be open to question in the event of an attractive-looking bid.

In 1982, BET Plc, the international services company, began a programme of major changes to move it away from being seen as a major takeover target with a market value of £240m to one which is now worth nearly £2bn and which turns over £2bn a year. The scale and nature of change both in the size and character of the business that BET planned for itself made the company concentrate on developing ways in which its new strategy could be communicated to shareholders and their support solicited in backing the company throughout the process.

Because the company was taking a long-term view, it wanted to identify those existing and potential shareholders who were also likely to take a long-term view and support the company throughout the changes. Its first task was therefore to look at the company's share register, see who was on it, and see how the balance of the register could be shifted to strengthen shareholder loyalty and support. The company was defining its audience.

The findings of BET's research into its share register and the actions which the company subsequently took provide a textbook example of the preparation which a company can make to avert disaster. They have been documented by BET's head of corporate communications, Neil Ryder, as Case Study 3 (see p.161).

If a company is performing below its perceived capabilities, it needs to convey that it does indeed know where it is going. A comprehensive presentation of the company's business strategy must be produced and communicated to all those concerned with the business. The shareholders, particularly the investing institutions, should be well informed. Externally, regular meetings with stockbrokers and journalists will lead to a better appreciation of the company and fewer nasty surprises.

It is also useful to carry out regular surveys of shareholder attitudes. If a benchmark study has been undertaken, a company will be better able to gauge shareholder perceptions by repeating surveys at critical moments.

Often a company will have a reasonable idea of the identity of a potential bidder. If this is the case, the company at the receiving end of the potential bid should check the predator's merchant bankers and stockbrokers against its own. In several recent battles it was discovered that the advisers to the two companies were the same. Valuable days will be saved in looking for new advisers if these are checked in advance.

Key data on which a successful defence could be based need to be regularly reviewed and updated. Included should be shareholder information, financial data per share, trading performance forecasts and the company's business strategy.

While shareholders' impressions of the company are likely to be a key factor in determining the outcome of the bid, the reputation of the company in the industry in which it operates can be as important a factor in determining whether a bid materializes. For example, if it became widely known that a company was badly managed, either generally or in one of the specialized fields such as finance, this could provide the motivation to launch a bid. For this reason, it is important that the company maintains a highly professional relationship in its dealings with other companies operating in the same industry.

Shareholders and others form their impressions about a company from meetings they may have with its representatives, from contact with other members of the financial community and from what they read in company documents, brokers' circulars and the media. All these points of contact are crucial and need to be reviewed from time to time to see if any improvements can be made.

Once a takeover bid has been announced, however, no company can anticipate a smooth ride, and expectation should be that the going will get rougher. As in war, strategy is the key to either a successful takeover or a successful defence.

'The vacuum caused by a failure to communicate is soon filled with rumour, misrepresentation, drivel and poison', said C. Northcote

Parkinson. The 'no comment' syndrome, especially in a crisis, is like a red rag to a bull.

Withholding information encourages speculation and often results in an inaccurate picture of the crisis building up. Worse, it can lead to accusations of a cover-up. Effective management of communication is as vital as effective management of the crisis itself. External perceptions about the crisis among key audiences will depend entirely on what they hear, see and read about it.

The key to managing communication in a crisis is for the organization at the centre of the crisis to establish itself quickly and firmly as the authoritative source of information about what is going wrong and the steps being taken to deal with the situation. It must be seen to be obviously willing and able to co-operate with the media and other external groups from the outset.

The first few hours of a crisis breaking, usually at bewildering speed, are the most difficult with which to deal. Likely as not, the company will have been caught on the hop and will have little it can communicate positively to the media until all the facts, and a first response, have been assembled.

Yet these early hours can be the most crucial if the company is to establish itself successfully as the single authoritative source of information. If it is not geared up to inform, it will be judged guilty until proved innocent. Companies must overcome a first instinct to remain silent, usually driven by concern over liability, uncertainty over who should speak, sometimes confusion over what really happened.

A company facing a crisis in a financial context can usually count itself luckier than one coping with an explosion at one of its plants 100 miles away being covered by reporters who know nothing about the industry, the company or the plant. If it has been doing its groundwork properly, it should have sound, continuing relationships with the financial correspondents and business editors covering its sector, as well as with analysts, institutional and private investors, professional advisers and so on.

Provided that these relationships do indeed exist, valuable time can be bought to assemble the first response. A company without such relationships, and the trust that goes with them, can expect to be treated harshly because no one knows anything about it.

The era when a Vanderbilt could say 'the public be damned' is gone. Today a company's health requires good relationships with customers, neighbours, employees, stockholders and suppliers, as well as with the media.

When bad news does break, the resulting corporate image contains negative factors. This may frequently result from a misinterpretation of events by the media but, whatever the cause, a retrospective look at the company's news-handling process in such cases usually indicates questionable judgement and inadequate preparation. No organization can afford to fail in this respect. The public is most likely to gain a bad impression if it perceives the organization to be unresponsive, confused, inept, reluctant or unable to provide reliable information.

Just as crisis can be anticipated and planned for, so can the organization's response be anticipated and planned for. This is the essence of crisis communication planning.

The consequences of not planning crisis communication are damaging to employees, to profits, to morale and to every other aspect of the organization. The consequences of any unplanned-for occurrence, however calamitous, can always be less costly and less traumatic when crisis communication is thoroughly planned in advance. When the unexpected happens, be sure to apply the cardinal rule of crisis communication: tell it all and tell it fast.

Journalists will be under fierce pressure to file their stories during a crisis. If you do not feed them the information they need, or you do not feed it swiftly enough, they will look for other sources, which may be less knowledgeable and reliable, but which will offer them their livelihood: a story.

The following actions must be taken if a company is to be able to communicate effectively in a crisis. Before the crisis occurs, proceed as follows:

1 Identify and maintain relationships with the media and other groups whose support will be crucial in a crisis situation.
2 Prepare background information packs on the organization and keep them up to date.
3 Establish a press room which can be used for press conferences and as a focal point where the media can collect the latest information.
4 Develop a cascade call-out list for all those designated and trained to facilitate communication during a crisis.
5 Set up an emergency press centre to take incoming calls from the media. Man it twenty-four hours a day if necessary.
6 Ensure that there are sufficient personnel within the organization trained to help cope with incoming media calls and calls from other external groups.
7 Ensure that the senior public relations representative is part of the crisis management team.

When the crisis occurs, continue as follows:

8 At the outset of a crisis, quickly establish a 'war room', and staff it with senior personnel trained to fulfil specific roles designed to

contain and manage the crisis, including the senior public relations executive.

9   Ensure the press office is kept up to date with developments as well as steps being taken to remedy the situation.

10   Set up telephone hotlines to cope with the floods of additional incoming calls that will be received. Have personnel trained to man them.

11   Know your audience and listen to their grievances. Ensure that you have a clear picture of their grievances against you. If possible, use research to verify your beliefs.

12   Get your opponents on your side by encouraging them to resolve the problem.

13   Add credibility to your cause by inviting objective, authoritative bodies to help end the crisis.

14   Always expect the unexpected. Be prepared to change plans, as things never go according to plan. Never underestimate the gravity of the situation.

15   Attach no stigma to employees who want to leave when a crisis occurs. Let them go: there are enough problems to cope with without having to look after less stable staff members.

16   Be prepared to cope with an extended period under a high level of pressure and stress, so do not exceed normal levels of alcohol and tobacco; reduce them if possible.

When communicating in a crisis, observe the following rules:

(a)   Start issuing background information about the organization as soon as possible after the onset of crisis, demonstrating your prepared-ness to communicate during the crisis, while providing valuable breathing space to prepare accurate press statements about what has gone wrong and what steps are being taken to remedy the situation.

(b)   Never speculate or tell untruths.

(c)   Issue new press releases as more known facts become available. Make sure others, to whom the press will be talking, also receive copies of the releases, so that everyone 'sings off the same hymn sheet'.

(d)   Announce the timing of press conferences as soon as possible to alleviate pressure from incoming calls. Prepare thoroughly for each press conference.

(e)   Remember the media do not work from nine to five. If the crisis is a major one, the company will be receiving calls from all around the world, from journalists operating in different time zones. Man the press office twenty-four hours a day, if necessary.

(f) If wrongly accused of a misdemeanour, leave no stone unturned in proving the accusation to be false.

(g) Wherever possible, look for ways of using the media as part of your armoury for containing the effects of the crisis.

(h) Develop a wide variety of information sources. Cultivate journalists and opinion formers. Keep up to date on reports on local radio, television and the press.

(i) In communicating about crisis, avoid the use of jargon. Use language that shows you care about what has happened and clearly demonstrates that you are trying to put matters right.

(j) Ensure that the organization has a list of responsible deeds and actions behind it to support the credibility of statements and claims made during the crisis.

10

International dimensions

Alan Macdonald

The internationalization of financial markets has transformed the communication needs, risks and opportunities for participants in those markets. Although seen most in the activities of securities houses, this phenomenon has also impacted on the two earlier exponents of overseas expansion: multi-national manufacturers and commercial banks.

Second only to the increase in coverage of financial affairs in the British national press and television has been the growth in overseas coverage, particularly from the United States and Japan, reflecting their central role as world financial markets. The *Financial Times* now has twenty bureaux overseas, with four correspondents in New York, three in Washington and three in Tokyo.

The *FT* Frankfurt edition sells nearly 60,000 copies and the New York edition 20,000; it is now printed at Roubaix, France, and will soon be printing in the Far East, probably Tokyo. The *Wall Street Journal*'s European and Asian editions now sell around 40,000 each. These newspapers and, to a lesser extent, the *International Herald Tribune* have had a much bigger impact on the globalization of news and its treatment than the clutch of cross-border magazines which preceded them. The circulations of the two most influential – *Institutional Investor* and *Euromoney* – appear to have peaked.

An even greater change has been seen in electronic publishing, with the invasion of the little green screens. As long as agency copy was carried on hard-copy printers, it was still largely raw material for tomorrow's newspapers. Now the international news agencies – Reuters, AP-Dow Jones, Knight-Ridder – transmit to dealers' desks and to the offices of financial decision-makers throughout the world. They can all see the same headline within seconds of the story breaking.

The next advance will be in television. America's Cable News Network, which specializes in covering business and financial news, is poised to improve its overseas coverage. NHK (Japan Broadcasting

Corporation) already has a daily direct feed from London. Both have link-ups with Channel 4's *Business Daily*.

Financial information of general news value can be transmitted by satellite and broadcast live or semi-live simultaneously across one or more continents. O Globo, based in Rio de Janeiro, has the largest audience of any television company in the world, with an appetite for news nearly as voracious as for 'telenovela' soap operas. A British banker door-stepped emerging from a debt-rescheduling meeting in the International Monetary Fund building in Washington might find himself on the *Money Programme* in the UK and cable television in the US but, by courtesy of O Globo, on prime time news throughout half of South America.

Besides news gathering, the main role for satellites has been in feeding cable systems. The present breakthrough is in trans-frontier direct broadcasting by satellite, which will soon be challenging terrestrial transmission, with a multiplicity of channels vying for European viewers.

Any organization operating internationally has to decide how it wants to be seen in each market in which it conducts its business. British Airways, Levi jeans and the Catholic church are exponents of the monolithic approach, enjoying the same manifestation of their corporate identity around the world. One reason for consistency of image may be economy of scale in the production of promotional material rather than any intrinsic advantage in linking users of distinct products in disparate markets.

There may, however, be clear advantages in being seen as a member of the local community rather than as an alien invader. Companies resist buying Peugeots for their fleets in the UK because of the nationality of the badge, even though these cars may have a higher UK content than British-sounding Vauxhalls. With the consumer it may be the other way round – which is why Currys invented the Matsui name to put on its British-made electronic goods.

Institutions may prefer to buy British securities from British market-makers, but Eurobonds and international equities from US or Swiss houses. This conundrum presented foreign acquirers of British stock-brokers with some difficult decisions in the run-up to Big Bang. Most have kept British identities in some form or another.

It is rare to find a successful retail banking operation which trades under a foreign name. The majority of British and Japanese banks in California kept the name of the bank they acquired to exploit the domestic potential, although some may have given as their rationale for the acquisition the strengthening of their global network. Equally, the only way for a foreign bank to be profitable in West Germany is to submerge its own national identity and appear to be a German bank.

These considerations apply to a greater or lesser extent wherever in the world banks have offices. The monolithic approach favoured by the US banks is usually the right one in major financial centres, which are linked one to another by the confluence of their markets. Foreign exchange is traded on a single global market, with the book passed from Tokyo to London to New York around the clock (and with windows for Sydney, Hong Kong and San Francisco).

Managing the wishes and whims of local managers around the world can be challenging. A rigorously enforced corporate identity system with clear rules on nomenclature, logos and typefaces is essential. But such a system should be capable of accommodating a diversity of local brands. It should also be sufficiently supple to allow for the endorsing of local identities, particularly in the case of joint ventures with partners applying a different set of rules.

Horror stories abound of English-language advertising copy appearing in vernacular media and of space booked on national holidays or in defunct publications or the wrong ones. The *Straits Times* in Singapore has frequently been the willing recipient of bookings intended for the *Business Times*, a quite separate newspaper.

Although perfectly respectable transnational campaigns can be created, they must be conceived from the start as such, taking into account local factors, and not just be add-ons to a domestic media schedule. Such campaigns are better suited to cross-border publications, notably the European and Asian editions of the *International Herald Tribune* and *Wall Street Journal*. But these, and the limited number of international magazines, appeal principally to US citizens and employees of US organizations.

There have been standard advertisements placed in indigenous media around the world from overseas – Japanese banks have been notable culprits – which have almost certainly done the perpetrators more harm than good. Quaint and alien themes and translations made in the country of origin deter, rather than encourage, business relationships.

Effective examples of foreign campaigns taken up by local agencies have been adaptations, not just translations. The ideal may be to provide local managers with the brief to the main agency and each advertisement in the series but to give them as much leeway as they need, allowing separate campaigns where local circumstances dictate.

There was a much-admired Citibank campaign in the early 1970s based on a domestic US theme: 'Sometimes you need a bank . . .' For example, the advertisement with the headline 'Sometimes you need a bank which puts the accent on Eurodollars', displaying accents from various European languages sitting on top of US dollar signs, was entirely appropriate to a US bank but very European in feel.

Overseas financial advertising requires a significant spend if it is to have any kind of impact against the weight of advertising of indigenous advertisers. A clear case can be made for advertising an office opening, a name change or a product launch, and for placing tombstones recording financial transactions. But even the value of advertising the parent company's annual results should be carefully weighed.

In some countries there are written or unwritten rules about the size and position, as well as the wording, of financial advertisements, to ensure that they comply with the norm established by or for the local players.

Generally, educating local managers in a fuller understanding of the public relations opportunities and responsibilities may prove a better investment than advertising.

For any financial institution, whose competitors are usually also its customers and often its regulators, fitting into its local business community is a necessity rather than a preference. Planned and sustained activity, which might include serving on committees, drafting technical papers to educate supervisors, speaking to study groups and writing articles for financial periodicals, should be regarded as essential duties for the officer in charge of the local operation. Visits of the chairman and other head office executives should be seen in this broader context, and should not be restricted to contact with managers and customers.

It is in this area that international sponsorship can prove effective, rather than just in reaching customers. Sponsorship can act as a short cut in creating a place for the sponsor within the local community, both in the sense of the association through the nature of the event and in the sense of useful shoulders that can be rubbed while the event is in progress. The supreme example in the UK is probably IBM's events programme, which is intended to demonstrate an American incomer to be a responsible UK corporate citizen.

Such a sponsorship need not take place in the target country. Midland Bank International's financing and underwriting of the Great Japan Exhibition at the Royal Academy in London in 1981 was aimed at the Japanese financial, business and government community rather than at the British public. The bank succeeded in achieving its objective by enabling Japan to achieve its own objective, which was to influence the attitude of the British public towards that country.

Preparing the ground in these ways can make a significant difference to the acceptance of a foreign company's business plans, including licence applications, acquisitions, disposals and lay-offs. At the very least it should ensure that the local manager knows which officials, legislators and other opinion-formers to seek out.

In communicating with staff in overseas locations it should be remembered that the local manager will be regarded by customers, counterparties and authorities as the plenipotentiary of his organization in every particular. He will therefore require information at the same time as it is released to the media on any major development, regardless of whether or not his divisional superior in head office is affected by it. This usually calls for a central information system, whether by electronic mail, multi-telexing or facsimile transmission.

On developments affecting his operations directly, he should expect to receive a call, preferably from the manager to whom he reports, before the news breaks and before he receives the release. It is sometimes difficult for local managers to understand that they cannot receive price-sensitive information in advance, which this courtesy should correct.

While the day-to-day internal communication function rests with the local manager, he can be supported in a number of ways from the centre.

An annual video explaining results and plans against shots of head office locations can even be appreciated by local staff who do not understand the language, if they are supplied with a written translation of the script and if the manager introduces it or stops and starts it to interject his comments.

So that local employees feel they are part of the corporate family, the manager should make it his responsibility to file stories for the staff newspaper. The editor may welcome what he will probably regard as colour pieces and place them prominently. The front page of *Midland Group News*, for example, has carried such pictures as the bank's Thai representative dressed to enter a monastic order, the bank's name and logo depicted in Javanese flowers, and Chinese dragons and tigers (various).

Visits, particularly by chairmen and chief executives, should be exploited to the full. The minimum should be dinner for the managers and their wives (not just the expatriates) and a party in the staff canteen, with a short speech commenting on financial performance and endorsing the local business strategy.

Communication with management and staff of an acquired company is a sensitive matter. The basic rule is only to communicate in the first instance through its own top management, who will relate to them in their own language and their own style. Material should be immediately sent to enable them to present information on your business – its history, organization and standing – to their own staff. But excessive familiarization may instil more despondency than delight.

Public relations agencies can prove valuable to overseas offices which cannot justify employing the requisite in-house skills, but the costs can be high, particularly in Tokyo and New York, where £5,000 might be regarded as a minimum monthly retainer. So a clear understanding of what is required of them is necessary.

The minimal requirement is that the agency can turn a news release round and fax major news items to head office immediately. Whatever their intentions, whether or not they have the expertise, overseas offices are unlikely to accomplish even this basic requirement themselves unless they have an individual seriously dedicated to the task.

An agency should also be able to seek opportunities for interviews for the local manager, specialists and head office visitors. This requires briefing on issues and rehearsing questions and answers, and should amount to more than just a diary function.

A consultancy can be a useful source of political and governmental information and can advise expatriate managers on local procedures and protocol. It should also be able to assist the manager in his local community role by suggesting contacts, by making introductions and by looking for external opportunities generally.

The ideal consultant is likely to be a local national or of the nationality of the colonial power. Apart from cultural considerations, expatriates usually stay for too short a time to have the necessary experience.

To succeed in co-ordinating an international public relations campaign there is no need for the agencies to belong to a single group. In small centres some agencies belong to several international groupings. The best policy is to choose the most suitable firm in the centre concerned and ask it to work with the others selected. It may make sense, however, for the client to appoint a co-ordinating office to cover the others in a region, whether these are on a retainer or merely ad hoc.

An overseas stock market listing can significantly raise the profile of the listed company, magnifying news, whether good or bad. Similar considerations apply to shelf registrations for Yankee bonds (US dollar bond issues by foreign companies in the domestic market).

The prescriptive disclosure requirements in the US have led foreign companies issuing bonds to detail more in their annual reports to bring them in line with their form 20Fs, filed annually with the Securities and Exchange Commission. As these documents are available to analysts and journalists, they would otherwise be providing less information to their shareholders at home than to overseas audiences.

The listing itself should be exploited to the full. There is no better opportunity to present an organization on its own terms to a financial community. A listing can enhance awareness of a company's products or services and create a base for local acquisitions.

In European countries raising visibility may in itself be a sufficient cause for the exercise. A presentation to a joint audience of analysts, institutional fund managers, customers and press, followed by a reception – at which they are handed an information pack containing the prospectus – is the standard practice.

The opportunity genuinely to broaden the shareholder base is much greater in the more liquid markets of the US and Japan, whether through issuing new shares or repackaging existing shares. The continuing requirements for quarterly reporting in the US and for translation of routine material in Japan are onerous and expensive, so no company should contemplate a listing on those stock exchanges purely for publicity purposes.

In Japan companies are advised to place themselves safely in the hands of their sponsoring securities house to ensure that they conform to local customs. The normal pattern would be briefings for press and analysts, in addition to a series of meetings with individual institutions to encourage them to invest, concluding with a mega-reception in a Tokyo hotel.

In the US the communication plan does not necessarily depend on which stock exchange has been selected for the quotation or on whether a full listing has been sought or an offering of American depository receipts (a repackaging of existing shares). The norm might be a roadshow to New York, Boston, Chicago, San Francisco and Los Angeles, with a security analysts' meeting in each to which the media may be invited (to fulfil the simultaneous disclosure requirements), as well as separate meetings with money managers. Investment bank advisers have a less upfront role than in Japan, but are the best route for reaching institutional investors.

The placing of shares on an overseas bourse, a takeover of an overseas quoted company or the buyout of minority shareholders can give rise to a considerable continuing responsibility for presenting to and answering questions from the financial press, analysts, fund managers, shareholders and, in the US, arbitrageurs (raiders who buy in anticipation of a move by a real predator). Apart from making regular visits, it is necessary to offer a local information point for news releases and to be ready to deal with eventualities arising from adverse brokers' circulars and from lawsuits, including class actions from groups of litigants.

Relations with the credit-rating agencies – Moody's and Standard & Poor's are the most prominent – should aim to minimize the impact of bad news. Rating agencies should receive news releases at the same time as the press and be contacted directly on any major development. Notice is given of changes in rating, so press spokesmen should be put on alert to take questions arising from downgradings.

The instant feedback from overseas of adverse or inaccurate coverage is essential. The rumour giving rise to the run on Continental Illinois Bank in Chicago arose in Tokyo.

When there is a false report that a company has closed down, given up a line of business, made a major loss or is guilty of criminal activity, it will not just be necessary to arrange a correction with the offending publication, but also to provide the correct information to other media, the authorities and clients. Where the inaccurate story is sourced to agency copy or to an accurate report of remarks by a third party, the publication may well decline to run a correction. The only answer may be to issue another story on the subject in question, thus demonstrating the inaccuracy of the previous report. An alternative may be an interview with the local manager. The London correspondent may be the best route for a correction, whether or not he perpetrated the error in the first place.

A serious rumour or leak or a real disaster may necessitate a more elaborate series of measures to be carried out by all employees in contact with the public. It is vital under these circumstances that any new developments are communicated instantly to all centres affected.

Close contact with the Foreign Office in London, and through the British embassy in the country concerned, with the relevant authorities in that country and with the foreign embassy in London may be required. Great sensitivity is necessary when a commercial organization is caught in diplomatic cross-fire as a result of its operations in such countries as South Africa, Libya and Argentina, particularly when its core domestic business is attacked by a political, religious or other pressure group.

There are more than 1,000 foreign correspondents in London from seventy-two countries, of whom about sixty-five exclusively cover financial news and many others include business as part of their general news coverage. Many use London as a base for reporting on all or part of continental Europe. There is no such concentration elsewhere in the world, even in the US, where they are split between New York and Washington.

Of the financial specialists, the *Wall Street Journal* and AP-Dow Jones should be seen as international rather than American, and their UK penetration should be taken into account. Agence France Presse also ranks as an international medium. Reuters should of course be regarded for its overseas coverage in addition to its dominant position within the UK financial community.

The German contingent is even more in evidence than the American, with *Handelsblatt*, *Frankfurter Allgemeine Zeitung* and *Borsen Zeitung* regularly reporting UK financial news. *Die Welt* is more concerned with economics, with thinner coverage on business matters. From Switzerland, *Neue Zurcher Zeitung* should be included for any major financial announcements. Of the Japanese media, the Jiji Press wire service and *Nihon Keizai Shimbun*, with its financial, industrial and English-language affiliates, have strong bureaux.

The Central Office of Information (COI) has a London correspondents' service, dividing them into groups covering finance, defence and science and technology (as well as culture). The COI organizes visits throughout the UK, including two or three a month for the financial group. It also arranges introductory programmes for newly arrived correspondents and occasional group visits for non-financial specialists wishing to know more about the City or business.

There are good opportunities for television and radio coverage. American television has an insatiable appetite for market comment against a dealing-room background. US broadcasters rely more on their sources to comment on the news than is the norm for British television. This fact can prove of great benefit for companies active in the US. Any organization that can offer interviewees speaking in the language of the television company concerned – and this also applies in radio, especially to the BBC Overseas Service – has a considerable competitive advantage.

Particular care has to be taken with the wording of releases intended for consumption in more than one country, especially where translation is necessary. This is a powerful argument for writing in simple English and for avoiding legal terms – not a consideration that legal and corporate finance advisers tend to take into account.

Where there is a joint release in two centres, for example for a takeover or joint venture, it may be preferable to have two separate versions rather than attempting a series of compromises. An alternative may be to place different quotations in otherwise identical releases or to switch paragraphs or the order of company names.

Translations should always be made in the country of destination by translators accustomed to writing for the press. They must be checked by an individual within the client organization with the technical knowledge to do so.

Special attention must be paid to the wording of the first sentence (and, to a lesser extent, the headline), as this will determine the headline on news printers and screens, which will have a significant impact on the tone of the coverage and how the story is picked up, passed on and used around the world.

No release should be drafted to build up gradually to its real point if there is to be any control of how the news is carried on the newswires.

The three principal routes for issuing news releases internationally – and all three should be exploited – are newswires, foreign correspondents and distribution in the country concerned. It is also possible to telex or fax overseas media directly as an alternative. Direct electronic input is not yet an option, although the London Stock Exchange's Topic service is received by the international wire services in London.

Any story of major significance will be carried on the wires worldwide. In Japan, for example, economic and financial news on AP-Dow Jones can run on Kyodo and items on Reuters can run on Jiji Press translated into Japanese. The wires will usually fulfil the disclosure requirement in the US, where simultaneous release is stipulated, rather than a requirement to advise stock exchanges in advance.

It is still worthwhile, however, to issue the full release in overseas centres, as Reuters, AP-Dow Jones and other agencies rarely carry stories in full. Standard & Poor's news service should be included in the US for company news. To ensure that the full version is transmitted in the US, where the media is dispersed across a continent, release through PR News Wire (in New York) and the Business Wire (in San Francisco).

When confidentiality allows, it is necessary to set the release up for issue in overseas centres, including translation, ahead of time. Otherwise the full version will be too late to compete with the newswire versions.

Where there is no public relations agency or competent local management or partner (for example, in an acquired company), a release can be telexed or faxed to key publications in that country, but they will only accept foreign language releases if they contain very important news. In London, Universal News Services (UNS) offers a commercial overseas service, with a scale of charges for reaching continents and individual countries.

Timing is a critical consideration. Drafters and approvers of press releases should be made aware that meeting deadlines may be more important than refining content.

It is necessary to determine priorities. Which country is the most important? When are the media deadlines? What are the opening hours of the stock exchanges affected?

With the new company news service of the International Stock Exchange in London it has become normal practice to release between 8am and 9am. This will not present a problem for the eastern and western seaboards of the US as long as you are geared up to release early in New York, preferably by 7.30am, when Dow Jones opens, and in time for the opening of the electronic over-the-counter market, Nasdaq (National Association of Securities Dealers Automated Quotations), at 9.00am and the New York and American stock exchanges at 9.30am.

In the case of a story originating in the US, even if released after the close of the New York and American stock exchanges at 4pm and 4.15pm respectively (Nasdaq at 5pm), it would still be possible to make the final editions of the UK press, if it is an important enough story. After 7pm or 8pm London time, primary responsibility for handling a US/UK story normally passes to the New York bureau of the *Financial Times*.

With a price-sensitive story, it is advisable to inform the specialist correspondents of the quality dailies after the Stock Exchange has closed that there is a major story coming, without giving any details. They can then decide whether to stay late or put their newsdesks on notice to alert them at home when the story breaks. If the news is good, it is clearly an advantage for it to be covered by the specialists; that way it will probably command more space. If the news is bad, there is a greater risk of inaccuracy resulting from lack of time or knowledge on the newsdesk.

In the case of a story originating in the Far East, where that market is considered of higher priority than the UK, it may be preferable to release during their working day, as long as it is issued after it is too late for the front and back pages of the *FT*, which can still take a major story up to 1am in the slip edition. If the item justifies it, it can be picked up in London on the 5.30am LBC (London Broadcasting Company) financial slot, the 6am BBC Radio news and the 6.45am BBC *Today* financial slot. So, to be on the safe side, the best expedient is to prepare to transmit to the exchange at 7am when the company news service opens.

The normal time for press conferences and interviews in Japan and Hong Kong is early to mid-afternoon, though Australia and Singapore are more in the British style of morning news gathering and afternoon writing. But, for a major development which is too price-sensitive for calling a press conference in advance, it is still feasible to call a conference at no notice for the late afternoon in Hong Kong.

In all these centres it is quite possible to release to coincide with London: 7am in London is 3pm in Hong Kong. Even 9am, if, say, there is a board meeting to give final sign-off at 8am, allows release at 5pm in Hong Kong, which is not too late. In Japan many national and regional dailies publish separate morning and evening editions; the deadline for the nationals is around noon for evening editions, but 1am for the morning, or an hour later for major news stories.

A danger of late release, however, is that the press is more likely to react to the versions of the story on the wire services. At best these may be based on the official release; at worst they may rely on an external source such as a government department, rating agency or analyst.

Another problem with late release is distribution. The latest reliable hand-delivery time in London is 4.30pm. So the combination of direct input to the London Stock Exchange, reading headlines, faxing and UNS will be necessary to achieve fast release after this time.

To stand a good chance of news being carried the following day in continental Europe, a release should be issued in London by 9am, if it is to be translated and issued that day. Dailies in West Germany require to receive releases by around noon. The latest time for filing from London is 1pm for most purposes, though hot news can be accommodated up to 6pm on most papers.

In seeking to handle public relations in overseas centres, full account must be taken of local practices.

In the US, for example, reporters do not often insert their own editorial opinions into copy, relying instead on quoting a number of different sources to build up a story. This method presents good opportunities for public relations practitioners, since they can put forward their clients as market commentators and, if they are sufficiently assertive and skilful, create attention for them out of proportion to the size of the organization.

But spokesmen have to proceed with extreme care, establishing ground rules before a conversation begins, or it may all be used on the record.

To understand press relations in Japan it is necessary to understand the press club system. There are about 400 clubs, each covering its own specific area, including government ministries, trade associations and political parties, which normally only make official announcements to an organized gathering of the members. News releases have to be issued through the appropriate club: for example, the Bank of Japan club for banking news and the Tokyo Stock Exchange club for securities. To distribute a release through a press club, permission has to be sought two days ahead from the club chairman. If it carries an embargo he has to agree the date and time.

Other than the trade journals and magazines outside the system, the Japanese media do not take a news release at face value, but contact the issuer or some other source for confirmation. To be sure that it will be covered, it is necessary to choose one newspaper and give it an exclusive interview. Unless familiar with the company concerned and the economy and financial system in which it operates, a reporter would not feel comfortable in interviewing its representatives, so it is vital to foster relationships with several reporters on each national daily.

In Hong Kong the Chinese press will print releases often more or less word for word as long as they are translated into Cantonese. But if there is a press conference, it is essential to invite the Chinese as well as the English-language media. If they are not invited, they may choose not to run the story unless it represents bad news.

On the other hand, in Singapore there are not enough papers to justify a financial press conference. The best plan is to talk directly to the *Business Times* (Singapore) and issue a release to the others, including the *Business Times* (Malaysia).

In West Germany business news stories are generally written in a neutral, show-the-figures way. Consistent with this style, quotes from company spokesmen are normally written in indirect speech. By contrast, editorial commentaries, based on the personal opinion of the author, can be more controversial than would be expected in the US or UK. But in many ways the German press is becoming more Anglo-Saxon in approach, with more flexible deadlines and less reliance on embargoes to cope with the pressures of the financial results conference season.

Understanding of the lasting cultural dimension of national quirks, customs and characteristics continues to determine success in the conduct of public relations internationally, just as much as the ability to keep pace with fast-moving global information and communication developments.

11

The role of corporate identity in managing change

John Smythe

In the seemingly hard-headed world of finance a question worth asking is whether corporate style, design and visual image can have any influence on purchasers of financial products, or on opinion-makers. For example, have they a role in the appeal to shareholders' loyalty in a bid contest?

There are three clear issues. Firstly, to what extent are our attitudes and opinions influenced by what we see? Do colour and form play a role in influencing our decision-making? Secondly, if it can be demonstrated that our sense of sight can play a persuasive role, how can form and colour be organized to support the commercial objectives of, say, an insurance company appealing to consumers, or an industrial conglomerate trying to influence its own shareholders and the opinion-formers who produce the share-buying climate? The third compelling question is whether the organized use of colour and form can be effectively managed to make an appreciable difference to a company's performance and, if it can, whether it is possible to measure the benefit.

A book on financial public relations is no place to expound on the accumulated research into the role of form and colour in shaping our understanding of the environment in which we live. It is sufficient to note that, with the sad exception of those blind from birth, everyone has an opinion about the appearance of everything, from the houses we live in to the cars we drive, the people we marry and so on. The arrangement of colour and form in any product or service is the trade, the craft and sometimes the science of design.

The key role of the successful designer (be it in graphics, buildings or products) is to identify contemporary taste or need and to design to appeal to or create taste. Successful identification of contemporary taste is more likely to result in a sale or a positive influence than is unsuccessful interpretation. Thus the successful designer fulfils an essential interpretative role before the act of design. Works of art might very well be spontaneous acts which take minimal cognizance of opinion and need. Design, on the other hand, is rarely undertaken without a clear need or, in the case of the business corporation, without a clear brief.

Let us see how this translates into the commercial world by taking a trip round a supermarket, before considering design's role in public relations.

When we think about going shopping for food products, we are probably driven by either necessity or whim. In the case of necessity we may not be too choosy about which outlet we go to or even the brand we buy. We assume the quality is acceptable, we check the price is within our limits and we make a hasty purchase decision. When indulging a whim, or when making a major decision, the criteria for choice that we apply probably become larger, more drawn out and, in shared households, democratic to a greater or lesser extent. In our minds the decision has become subject to what we hope is a sensible trial by reason and logic conducted by a fair-minded jury – and, to the extent that the different criteria are weighed in competition, it is.

If we look more closely at those criteria – price, quality, service, location, safety, experience, familiarity, ethics of the product or manu-facturer and so on – we find that we perhaps review each of them in turn, then aggregate them and reach a decision by the very human process of negotiation, in which criteria seemingly unrelated to the immediate purchase, such as life-style, subconsciously feature. So what seems to be a rational decision-making process is actually driven strongly by our experience of what is right for each one of us. This helps to explain why some people will only shop at a Tesco store, while others would not go anywhere near one; and why some new, highly-priced delicatessen style outlets can succeed where the cheaper, ordinary corner shop fails.

Why is it so? Quite simply because most of us tend to make relatively safe decisions based on personal identification with a product or a service. We say such things as 'This feels like us' or 'This is my style'. We learn and are positively encouraged by the media and by peer example to identify with certain products, services and life-styles, even with countries and with different types of people.

We identify with companies and products and services by the same processes as we identify with other aspects of our lives. It follows that our experiences of and level of familiarity with a particular company or brand will figure largely in how positively we rate them.

Books on public relations are fond of making the point that the process of creating familiarity among influential audiences is one that can be managed through a planned communication programme. Design – the process by which mankind organizes and arranges colour and form – plays a powerful role both in shaping our physical environment and in providing the professional communicator with one of the keys to reaching a consumer or decision-maker's sense of sight and thus influencing the choices they make.

The second question is whether form and colour can be organized through design to support the commercial objectives of an organization, and, if so, how and when it can be done.

People have names, appearances and forms of behaviour which act as signals and codes for the rest of the world to read their intentions and mood. Companies also express themselves in similar ways through their:

- Communication.
- Behaviour of staff.
- Appearance.
- Names.
- Property and environment.
- Ethical standards.

Communication includes all paid-for advertising and the messages that come over in editorial press comment derived from press relations.

The behaviour of staff, from the chairman to the most junior employee, is the most direct impact which an organization has on the world in which it operates. Many of us will have experienced the difference between travelling on a British Airways flight and travelling on those of many of its competitors. BA's recent commitment to staff training is self-evident.

A company's *appearance* is also physically on show through artefacts such as printed material, signs, liveries and such corporate memorabilia as giveaways.

An organization's *names* are powerful descriptive signals to the outside world. Names are attached to legal entities, divisions, departments, companies, brands and other more transitory collections of people or assets, including working parties and committees. Sometimes they help people find their way around the organization; sometimes they hinder.

The *outward appearance* of factories, retail outlets, offices and other property also conveys strong images to staff and visitors alike. You would not, for example, find much out of place in a manufacturing facility belonging to IBM, Boeing or Mercedes. The reception areas of the average general medical practitioner, British Rail ticket offices or the benefits department of a Department of Health and Social Security office, on the other hand, leave you in no doubt of the esteem in which their callers are held.

The *values and ethics* of an organization often become clear when mishaps occur, in how the company reacts to an environmental or safety problem, or the actions it takes when a product proves to be dangerous or ineffective. The organization can only react positively if it has developed policies on all the issues which its operations might raise.

All these manifestations of an organization's personality give an indication of what it is or what it is trying to be. They can all be either left unmanaged or positively used as a valuable management tool. That tool goes under the name of corporate identity. When managed positively, corporate identity helps an organization, or a product, to emerge clearly in front of the competition.

Sadly, the responsibility for communication, behaviour, appearance and the other characteristics of corporate identity is too often fragmented among a variety of different departments in an organization, and the chances of achieving a coherent identity are slim. Thus the first step to managing identity is to encourage an understanding of all the elements contributing to an organization's image.

Secondly, communication, property and the other components of identity must be co-ordinated either through strong central control or, where a more devolved management structure prevails, by the adherence to simple rules and policies and a strong communication culture to bind the group together.

Identity programmes receive press coverage when major companies like Prudential or ICI make a radical change to their visual image. Headlines focus on the shiny new logo, while the editorial ruminates on the cost of the design process. The impression given is often one of a one-off exercise, a flash in the pan. In reality, the creation of a new identity can be a lengthy process, taking up to five years, and its subsequent management is a management function with the same requirement for continuity as any other.

The creation of a corporate identity programme involves a clear sequence of events.

Firstly, one must identify the need. Most managements feel they have an identity problem when their business is in a period of change. Symptoms might include market growth or stagnation, the threat or prospect of takeover, internationalization and other structural changes in the organization's marketplace, such as major developments in technology.

A change in circumstances necessitates a modification of the business plan and thus inevitably of the organization's identity. Failure to react may result in takeover and the possible break-up or demise of the business.

Secondly, one must investigate the need. That is the first step in an identity programme. Good practice is to undertake a qualitative research programme by a team of business, communication and design consultants. A series of discussions are held throughout the client organization, from the board to the shopfloor, and externally among influential groups, from customers to the local community and including key financial audiences. The objectives of the discussions are broadly to:

1   Determine facts about the size, shape and profitability of the business and its constituent parts.
2   Assess the organization's strengths, weaknesses and areas of specialization, and determine the historical reasons for the status quo.
3   Assess the relationship between the existing name structure and the management structure.
4   Determine prevailing perceptions of management style and vision.
5   Conduct an audit of all printed material to assess what messages are conveyed to readers.
6   Determine what channels and tools are utilized to communicate internally and externally, and their effectiveness.
7   Review the organization in the context of its competition, customers and the opinion-formers in its industries.
8   Evaluate existing ethics and corporate values in the organization in relation to the industry in which it operates.

The number of people interviewed can vary from a dozen for a small-scale study to several hundred for the investigation of a large, complex conglomerate.

Following these discussions, the multi-disciplinary investigation team determines the principal issues facing the business. These might range over:

(a)   The power of its roots and history.
(b)   The style of management.
(c)   The state and prospects of the industry in which it operates.
(d)   The strength and clarity of the organization's *raison d'être* or market proposition.
(e)   The power, or otherwise, of its visual identity.
(f)   The appropriateness of existing marketing and communication activities.
(g)   Public issues, such as whether its operations are running foul of public opinion and are thus liable to consumer or legal backlash.

The process of investigation and analysis can take between one and four months. It is designed to allow both the client organization and the consultancy to take a hard look at the real issues facing the business, for both to be seen to consult widely and to enable them to develop a common basis for working together.

The chief executive officer and a small steering group would then normally work with the consultancy to agree how the investigating team's findings and the issues which have been raised can be developed as a brief to effect change in the organization. If identity is the process by which corporate strategy can be clarified and projected, it stands to reason that the process of change will embrace much more than graphics, architecture and publications.

But these are simply the artefacts of change. Before any can become useful tools, the issues raised by the investigation – perhaps covering strategy, structure, markets, management, individual managers, marketing and public issues – need to be discussed in the context of the organization's own plans for change, where these already exist.

Where organizational and structural issues prevent the achievement of the business strategy, the task force will need to decide which of these issues to address themselves, and when to ask for additional assistance, perhaps from a strategically orientated management consultancy or an in-house team. For example, a recent Smythe Dorward Lambert study on identity and communications for a major British firm found that the organization's pattern of growth by acquisition had resulted in the creation of a federal group with little binding the parts together apart from finance. The consequences were limiting in terms of both image and opportunities. A fragmented image meant that important audiences, such as institutional shareholders and the City press, had difficulty in understanding the full picture, and thus the organization was only being judged on the parts that were perceived to be connected, not on the whole.

As for business, the company's federal structure, despite some benefits for the small business units, prevented single major markets like the motor industry or the aerospace sector being attacked by a single, more powerful force. As a result the company was unable to interpret properly or respond to major trends in procurement, and was thus not able to sustain research and development activity sufficiently to keep up with the market. It found itself with products which filled disparate niche markets, and the company was considered to be a supplier of components, rather than an organization providing systems solutions to complex manufacturing problems.

It is clear from this example that corporate identity cannot be separated either from business strategy (plans for developing a market) or from organizational structure (the way a company organizes itself to achieve the plan).

Once issues relating to strategy and the shape of the business have been resolved, the first plans to implement and communicate change can be laid.

Armed with sufficient knowledge of the client company's industry, its position in that industry and in different geographical markets, and the proposed way of doing business, the consultancy can set to work on writing a positioning document. This serves as a brief for the implementation team of designers, behaviouralists and communicators. As well as summarizing strategy, the positioning paper defines the desired reputation to be created for the company or product.

Reputation can be summed up as the prevailing consensus view about an individual or a company. Everybody and every company has a reputation. Reputation can be changed to reflect new behaviour – either slowly or quickly and powerfully. Individuals, perhaps as a result of peer pressure, decide for themselves and make their own changes. Companies need help to change their way of doing things and to communicate that change.

The analytical phase of an identity programme is designed to present the options for change. The implementation stage is the part of the process where the disciplines and tools of change are put to use. Each requires special skills and the plan requires tight co-ordination.

The role of the designer is to interpret the written description of the organization's strategy and proposed reputation and to develop a visual style which will encapsulate and endorse both strategy and reputation. This is only achievable when designers are a part of the investigating team, as they must be if they are to complement the consulting process.

Usually, a series of design options is created before agreement is reached by the client's board or top management. Solutions must of course be based on the criteria developed in the brief rather than on the chairman's personal taste! Acceptance of change is never easy and a radical repositioning of a company (or brand) will require a bold solution.

Prudential's new visual symbol, although derived from the corporation's founding idea of 'prudence', was none the less a radical move (Figures 11.1 and 11.2). So was the design work for 3i (Figure 11.3), formerly ICFC (Industrial and Commercial Finance Corporation), and the new petrol brand developed for Kuwait Petroleum (Figure 11.4) when that company acquired many of Gulf Oil's European stations and needed to establish rapidly a presence in a highly competitive market. By contrast, the design work undertaken for ICI (Figure 11.5) represents a subtle shift of emphasis. Bovis's 'hummingbird' is shown in Figure 11.6.

An identity or house style may consist of a symbol or logo, guidelines on the usage of colour and typeface and a naming structure and associated logotypes. A thoroughly implemented visual identity has to be developed to use on every piece of print or artefact the organization uses, from an aeroplane to a letterhead. The blueprint for all these manifestations is then captured in an identity manual.

Detailed design work may take anything from one month to four or five years to complete, depending on the size of the organization and the pace of change required. Overnight changes may be less expensive but they lack the element of visual shock, which makes the task of powerfully communicating the rationale behind the changes more difficult.

Figure 11.1 *In one of the most comprehensive UK corporate identity programmes of recent years a personification of prudence was used to reflect the qualities of financial services group Prudential Corporation in a contemporary way, capable of a multiplicity of applications (created by Wolff Olins)*

Figure 11.2

Figure 11.3 *Industrial and Commercial Finance Corporation became known as ICFC, then was renamed Investors in Industry. Now it is simply 3i, the name and the style both coming from the designers (created by Wolff Olins)*

Figure 11.4　*The visual pun, sensibly used, can be a way of creating high impact, especially as here where the brand identity and the structure have been designed together for Kuwait Petroleum's European operation (created by Wolff Olins)*

Figure 11.5　*When the corporate symbol, subtly updated over the years, is as well established as ICI's, little more is needed for an international outdoor advertising campaign*

Figure 11.6   *With a bold name presentation even a delicately detailed symbol can be effectively applied to heavy construction equipment, as Bovis demonstrates (created by Wolff Olins)*

That communication task should not be underestimated. It is all too tempting to let the visual identity speak for itself, which of course it cannot. The identity will not start to work positively for the organization until the rationale for change has been communicated, particularly to those within, and the real changes to the organization have started to be implemented.

Disinformation can be a powerful enemy. From the outset of the investigation stage the communication process is ignored at the peril of the project. It needs careful handling to manage expectations, particularly those of middle management. The underlying purpose of the identity task in hand requires proper explanation both at the outset and throughout the process.

It virtually goes without saying that the identity will require launching, both inside and outside the company. The emphasis should be on an explanation of the rationale behind the programme, with great care being taken to introduce the ideas to the many different internal audiences, providing differing levels of detail according to the appetite of the group. The form of the information exercise can vary from a discrete written paper to multi-media conferences.

The objectives of communicating to staff are to ensure the desired level of understanding and continued commitment to the organization, and to equip them to transmit the message inside and outside the company.

In addition to preparing for the launch of the identity, the initial investigation will have thrown up issues relating to how and what the organization communicates, internally and externally, on a day-to-day basis. In some cases it becomes clear that the organization will not be able to sustain the new communication effort in the long run, and it will be necessary to create a new function backed by appropriate resources.

It may also be opportune to review whether the existing public relations or public affairs department requires the addition or change of skills. For example, few in-house departments are currently skilled in public issues analysis, and fewer still are able to initiate changes to an organization's corporate ethics and values policy.

An organization's staff is its most valuable resource, so, in addition to the communication exercises, it will almost certainly be necessary to alter motivational and behavioural work attitudes at the top, middle and lower levels. Top management may well have to be persuaded to think in a more group-orientated way, rather than simply defending their own patches. Middle managers may have to transfer this broadened attitude to sales staff, for example.

Lower levels may be required to adopt completely new patterns of behaviour towards customers, as in the British Airways programme. This all requires specialist training and perhaps an amended reward structure to provide incentives.

None of all these can be as effective as they should if the environments in which staff work, or that customers visit, do not reflect the business and cultural changes that are taking place.

Organizations can manage their corporate identity to their advantage – provided that the process goes deeper than the visual image, is communicated properly and, lastly, is managed in the long term like any other management resource.

The final question of whether the benefits of a corporate identity programme can be measured requires some definition. Awareness of a new brand or a new product can be measured by research and at the cash register. A share issue sells or does not. A company's success, on the other hand, can really only be measured if it achieves its strategic objectives, be they to survive, grow, diversify or whatever.

That being so, the corporate identity programme must be a part of the process of contriving change, so that the company achieves its objectives. If it does, the identity programme has been a success. If not, it was probably not considered as part of a strategic process and deserves to fail.

Case Study 4 (p.166) deals with the establishment of a new identity for the Dutch chemicals giant, Akzo.

12

Measuring opinion

Peter F. Hutton

Traditionally the public relations industry has relied on relatively informal and often unsystematic methods of collecting opinions: drawing up a list of contacts and meeting them for periodic informal discussions, monitoring editorial coverage in newspapers and magazines, and so on. Clearly such methods have a vital part to play in establishing important relationships and feeding a reservoir of background knowledge. But they also have their limitations. They are highly vulnerable to subjective interpretation and lack the objectivity which the systematic sampling, standardized questioning and numerical data analysis techniques of the survey researcher provide.

Professional practitioners of public relations have increasingly turned to more scientific methods to complement other information-gathering activities. These techniques allow for the production of graphical and numerical comparisons, based on a survey taken in a concise period of time and, equally important, enable the extent of change to be measured between surveys taken weeks, months or even years apart.

In many areas survey research can:

1 Provide a framework of perceptions within which to define the objectives of a programme of public relations.
2 Identify the most effective means of executing such a programme.
3 Evaluate the degree to which the programme has been effective in meeting its objectives.

Research is applied to virtually every audience of interest to financial public relations practitioners. These audiences will vary according to the client, but are likely to include the City, private shareholders, customers and employees.

The seriousness with which financial public relations is now taken in the City reflects a boardroom realization that Stock Exchange activity and share price movements are not just the result of reactions to published financial results, or to market factors beyond the control or influence of the company itself. How messages are conveyed, to whom and in what context are as important as the messages themselves, and it is the role of skilled practitioners of financial public relations to manage these factors to the best advantage of their clients or employers.

In this context the term 'City' usually refers to a relatively small group of highly influential people, mostly located in or around the City of London, although some may be found in the regional financial and commercial centres, such as Edinburgh, Glasgow or Manchester. They are the institutional investors and the equity managers of major insurance companies, pension funds and unit trusts, stockbrokers' analysts and the leading business and financial journalists.

A sound understanding of a company and a good reputation will increase its attractiveness as an investment, help to stabilize its share price, reduce its vulnerability to takeovers and increase the credibility of its communications. In an environment which is highly sensitive to rumour and innuendo, being well known and well regarded has become a key objective for many major companies.

Any in-house or consultancy public relations executive is severely handicapped in his or her activities in the City without the answers to a number of basic questions:

(a) How well is the company known?
(b) How favourably or unfavourably is it regarded?
(c) What are its perceived strengths and weaknesses?
(d) How were these derived?
(e) How do City audiences primarily evaluate the company?
(f) How accurate is their knowledge about such things as the company's activities, its management and its financial track record?

These questions normally provide the basic starting point for research among City audiences.

Since 1969 MORI has measured the reputation of many of the major quoted companies in Britain among business and financial journalists and since 1982 among institutional investors and stockbroking analysts. For example, Figure 12.1 plots companies according to how well they are known by institutional investors (using mean scores derived from a five-point familiarity scale) and how favourably or unfavourably they are regarded (using scores from a five-point favourability scale). The line of best fit suggests that the better known companies tend to be better regarded – familiarity breeding favourability – although of course companies can quickly become known for the wrong reasons!

Similarly, Figure 12.2 shows the reputation of four companies among institutional investors as measured in the autumn of each year from 1982 to 1987. It shows how Glaxo consistently managed to maintain an extraordinarily favourable reputation over this period, with Smith & Nephew not far behind. By contrast GEC's pre-eminent reputation in

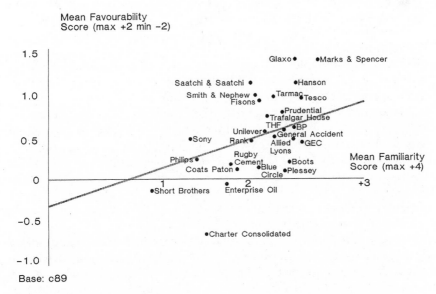

Figure 12.1   *Company familiarity and favourability among institutional investors, 1985*
Source: MORI

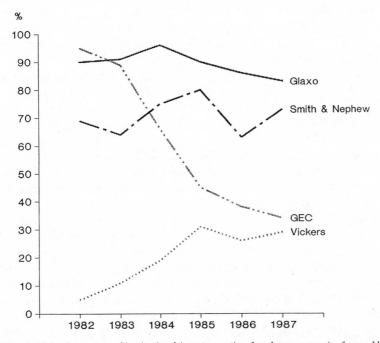

Figure 12.2   *Percentage of institutional investors rating four large companies favourably*
Source: MORI

1982 was eroded year by year. Vickers started from a low base and gradually built its reputation in the City.

Company reputations are best perceived relatively. In Figure 12.1 Glaxo and Marks & Spencer, for instance, are perceived favourably relative to other companies in their sectors and relative to major companies as a whole. GEC is rated more highly than Plessey but less highly than companies in other sectors which are equally well known.

Marked changes in reputation should be viewed in the context of changes in the reputations of other companies in the sector and of companies as a whole. The MORI 1987 City Opinion Survey, taken in the autumn of that year, showed, for example, a strong decline since the previous spring in the favourability ratings accorded by institutional investors to nearly every company measured following the October 1987 stock market crash. In that context a slight decline was actually a relatively favourable finding.

While institutional investors wield power through buying and selling large blocks of shares, stockbrokers' analysts have great influence in the City. One recent survey found that 91 per cent of institutional investors regard analysts as their main source of information about individual companies. While institutional investors would normally include stock from a wide variety of sectors in their investment portfolios, analysts will normally specialize in one sector or in a very few. They will study companies in those sectors closely and will be in a better position than anyone else to evaluate a company's performance and prospects, its strengths and weaknesses.

In assessing a company, research has shown that it is at least as important to be seen to have the right management as to have a good financial performance. In the minds of analysts the two are highly interrelated. A company's profitability depends upon its managerial ability to deliver. If it fails to read market changes, is structured wrongly to respond appropriately, fails to set clear objectives in line with optimizing its profitability or is plagued by industrial disputes or non-productive boardroom clashes, then analysts are likely to mark it down, and the stock market will follow.

Business and financial journalists play a crucial role both in disseminating information and in influencing opinion. Their choice of running favourable or unfavourable stories about a company or the interpretation they choose to place on those stories will inevitably influence the opinions of those who read them. Moreover, their influence extends well beyond the City and will affect shareholders, employees, customers, suppliers, business opinion-leaders and competitors.

The UK government's programme of privatizing state assets has meant that whereas in 1983 only one person in fourteen held shares in a private company, four years later this had risen to one in five.

The effect has been not only to more than triple the market for direct shareholder communication (the majority of new shareholders hold shares in two or more companies), but also to increase the number of people who are targeted for direct mail or financial advertising (unit trusts, personal equity plans, etc.) and the number who are potentially exposed to indirect forms of financial communication.

Research has shown how new ownership of shares has increased the public's reading of the financial pages of their newspapers, their propensity to discuss their investment with their peers and their willingness to read advertisements aimed at them.

An effective shareholder relations programme needs to be based on a sound knowledge and understanding of shareholders and their needs. Without research most companies are dependent on comments made and questions asked by the handful who turn up to their annual meetings, or the letters they receive. Since AGM attenders and letter writers are both likely to be the more opinionated and the holders of the more extreme views, they are an unreliable – indeed highly misleading – source of shareholder opinion.

The only other information such companies will have about their shareholders is that which they can derive from the share register. This consists of little more than the number of shareholders, the size and type of their shareholding and their names and addresses.

This is hardly sufficient information on which to base an investor relations' programme. It says nothing about what shareholders know about the company, their attitudes towards it, their information needs or their reactions to information they receive by direct mail or via press coverage. It says nothing about their commitment to the company, the reasons why they bought, will hold or may sell their shares, or whether the investment being made in investor relations is worthwhile or how it might be improved. For most companies it is little more than a convenient mailing list and the source of information for that little table at the back of the annual report that states how many shareholders own various numbers of shares.

To the researcher, however, it provides an ideal listing for drawing a representative sample of shareholders for a survey which can provide all this information, and much more, to aid investor relations.

The objectives of an investor relations programme will vary according to the company and prevailing circumstances, but such a programme might aim to:

1   Build up the confidence of shareholders in the business and its management.
2   Provide a positive and realistic perspective within which to view the company's performance.

3   Provide the basis for effective and efficient communication.
4   Establish a high level of trust, credibility and loyalty.
5   Develop and maintain a strong and positive corporate image.

Normally such surveys are conducted by telephone, which works well so long as shareholders are warned by a letter from the company that an approach will be made. Postal surveys should be avoided, because of the low response rate, and the near certainty that the replies will come from the shareholders with strong and often extreme views.
Research is generally used to:

(a) Monitor satisfaction with share performance.
(b) Ascertain the reputation of the company and its management.
(c) Assess the degree of knowledge shareholders have about the company.
(d) Identify newspaper and magazine readership to discover how to reach shareholders and potential shareholders indirectly.
(e) Assess recall of, and reactions to, the annual report.

The sheer scale of privatizations such as British Telecom and British Gas have meant that relatively straightforward shareholder communication, in a number of cases to more than a million shareholders, can be massively expensive in printing and mailing. In this context research provides vital information to improve the cost-effectiveness of decision-making. Research for British Telecom, for example, was able to give early reassurance that only a tiny proportion of its 1.6m shareholders were likely to attend their first two annual general meetings and nearer the date was able to predict with remarkable accuracy the actual turnout at each event.

Other periodic research for British Telecom has aided its shareholder relations programme by providing information on topics such as buying and selling intentions, shareholder motivation, shareholder satisfaction, ownership of other shares, BT social policy, future expectations, BT corporate image, newspaper readership, readership of the annual report, advertising awareness and recall, awareness of sources of advice, and usage of and satisfaction with the BT shareholder enquiry service. Some of these measures have been taken a number of times in different surveys to provide an indication of how shareholders' attitudes and behaviour are changing.

The last few years have seen a spate of contested takeovers in which the small shareholder has played a crucial role. In Britain the proportion of a company's shares held by the small investor rather than institutions averages around 25 per cent, but with some companies can be much higher. The takeover bid for Spillers some years ago was a particularly protracted affair, in part because 70 per cent of the shares were owned by small shareholders. But even if small shareholders own only 20 per cent of the shares, this may still be crucial to winning the vital 51 per cent control.

It is when a hostile takeover bid for a company is made that all the effort put into establishing sound shareholder relations suddenly becomes important. There are certain things the company needs to get right, and research can be used to measure its success in doing so. If it has been successful, shareholders will be much more likely to remain loyal to the company, will have confidence in the company's management and will be far more likely to set store by any communication it receives from the company in preference to those from the predator.

When a bid is actually made, good financial public relations is essential. The purpose on each side is to convince the shareholders that the bid or the defence is preferable, and to persuade them to follow the course of action recommended. The need for quick and reliable information is crucial to see where you stand in the 'ideological war', and what you have to do in order to win it long before the acceptances start to come in.

The outlay on the campaign for or against is likely to run into hundreds of thousands and, in some cases, millions of pounds. By comparison, the outlay on research is trivial, yet the potential savings from making better, because more informed, decisions is enormous.

Such research is used to identify:

- Awareness of the bid and bidder.
- Likelihood of acceptance.
- Factors which will determine acceptance or rejection.
- The degree to which messages being put out by both sides are heard and believed by shareholders.
- The influence of top executives, particularly the chairman.
- Corporate reputations.
- Readership: which papers shareholders read and which financial journalists' views they believe.

Regular telephone research can provide updates on a weekly or, if necessary, daily basis to help define strategy and monitor tactical problems. Research early on can, and does, provide a vital blueprint for what needs to be done in communication terms to achieve the desired goal.

In one takeover battle a survey undertaken for a predator among its victim's shareholders showed that, not only did 29 per cent rate its offer as 'poor' compared with only 5 per cent who thought it was 'good', but shareholders gave their own company markedly better ratings in terms of its performance, the quality of its management and the advice given by its directors, than they did to the well-known predator. In other words, the predator was starting with a major reputation problem which had to be overcome if it was to stand a chance of succeeding. Shortly afterwards it threw in the towel.

The programme of privatization of state assets since 1979 has also provided major new opportunities for the financial public relations industry. The British Telecom flotation – at the time the largest ever undertaken – did more than just sell BT shares. It succeeded in breaking the savings patterns of a lifetime of more than 1m people in Britain. More than half had never owned shares in a private company before; they also tended to be younger and less middle-class than the average traditional shareholder.

This, and the other privatization marketing campaigns, succeeded in convincing people that buying shares need be no more difficult than opening a bank or building society account. They discovered that shareholding is not just for a rich élite with access to a stockbroker, and that it is now socially acceptable to be a shareholder even if you are working class and vote Labour.

All the major privatizations have called extensively on research – both qualitative and quantitative – to define the communication objectives, test promotional literature and documentation, and monitor awareness, interest and attitudes over time. Research has provided the vital link between the communicator and the recipient of communications in the process of establishing *awareness*, cultivating *interest*, creating *involvement* and turning this into share purchase *action* (see Figure 12.3).

Over the last decade there has been an increasing move towards informing employees about the financial position of the organizations they work in. Heightened concern during the 1970s about Britain's relative industrial decline focused attention on the fact that most employees had little understanding of, and lacked commitment to, the factors which led to the financial success of the companies they worked for. In the 1980s there has been a trend towards greater financial involvement of employees through profit-sharing schemes and employee share ownership. The privatization programme has given a fillip to this by providing sufficient incentives to ensure that a large proportion of employees in most privatized concerns became shareholders.

However, while a number of companies run highly successful employee share ownership schemes, and will testify to the substantial benefits in terms of employee commitment and motivation, the majority have not yet absorbed the basic principles of such schemes into their corporate cultures. Of those that have, many are still feeling their way in terms of determining the most appropriate form of financial public relations for the internal audience.

Research has been applied in a number of ways to help companies to communicate financial information to employees, whether or not they are shareholders. Often information is drawn from a more general

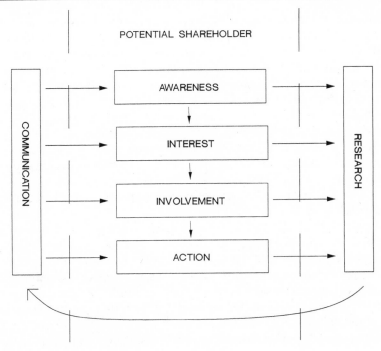

POTENTIAL SHAREHOLDER

COMMUNICATION

AWARENESS

INTEREST

INVOLVEMENT

ACTION

RESEARCH

Figure 12.3   *The process of share buying.*

survey of employee opinions to gauge employee understanding of the financial position of their company; their sense of commitment to, or responsibility for, helping the company to achieve financial success; the sources of information found most useful for keeping informed about the company; and receipt of, interest in and readership of reports to employees.

However, it is probably true that while a great number of companies do make an effort to communicate their financial results to employees, either through an internal newspaper, a year-end employee report or by means of videos, they rarely research the effectiveness of these media in transmitting information or changing attitudes.

One company which used a video to communicate to its employees the fact that it had made a loss the preceding year and to rally support for rectifying this, found that fewer than half those who had seen the video took away with them the basic message, and 47 per cent actually thought it had made a profit! The research highlighted important weaknesses of the medium and enabled the company to review its approach to communicating financial messages to its employees, thereby increasing the effectiveness of its public relations investment.

A number of companies have targeted employee shareholders (normally including ex-employees, pensioners and often spouses and other relatives) for special financial public relations attention and have used research to evaluate the effectiveness of their programmes. Research for H P Bulmer, for example, found that 84 per cent of its employee shareholders had at least glanced at the annual report, and some 29 per cent had claimed to have read all or most of it. Surveys conducted for other companies allowed this to be put in perspective. It suggested that Bulmer's readership was slightly better than the norm.

Shareholders also found the report informative, with half of those who had read it rating it as 'very informative' and some 40 per cent 'fairly informative'. Again, studies among other shareholders enabled this to be put in perspective and suggested Bulmer's rating was exceptionally good. 'Very informative' scores for other companies ranged from 40 per cent down to as low as 19 per cent.

The survey also allowed Bulmer to examine its reputation in a number of other dimensions. Nearly nine out of ten rated its communication with shareholders as good and only 2 per cent poor. Two out of three rated the quality of management as good and only 4 per cent poor. Two-thirds also rated its treatment of employees as good and only 1 per cent poor. The highest 'poor' rating was for its financial performance, but even here the 'good' ratings outweighed the 'poor' ratings by six to one.

The National Freight Consortium is not a typical company, because it has 30,000 or so employee shareholders, and it has used research for a variety of unusual applications to assess their views. These have included assessing likely numbers at its extraordinarily well attended annual general meetings, and ascertaining shareholders' opinions on a number of strategic questions such as:

- Whether their share ownership should be extended to a number of employees not included in the scheme.
- Future corporate development strategies.
- Flotation of the company on the Stock Exchange.

Research showed that the board basically had the backing of its shareholders for floating the company and also identified anxieties about the flotation, which needed to be addressed by a communication programme.

Clearing banks, building societies, insurance companies and unit trust organizations all make extensive use of market research to help them define consumer needs for financial products and services and related communication. The breakdown of the barriers between the services offered by the clearing banks and building societies has led to an extraordinary effort by both types of institution to market their products and build strong corporate images, frequently stressing efficient and friendly service to the customer.

The clearing banks and insurance companies also serve the needs of corporate customers, along with accountancy firms and, at the top end of the market, the merchant banks. Stockbrokers serve the needs of the more affluent small personal investor, as well as the professional fund manager.

Opinion research has been used to assist in the marketing and promotional efforts in the corporate sector of all these types of organizations, but particularly the clearing banks. Their concern has been to establish a reputation for being professional and approachable, providing the kind of services the corporate customer needs at reasonable cost.

To support this the clearing banks have rapidly increased the range of services available to corporate customers and developed a far greater marketing orientation at branch level while setting up pockets of local, regional or central expertise designed to support the specialized needs of business. Research has been a vital element in this process by providing information to establish and maintain the marketing strategy.

Thus far the emphasis has been on survey research – the use of a standardized questionnaire administered to a representative sample of a defined population, be it institutional investors, stockbroking analysts, financial journalists, small shareholders, employees or customers. The questions will normally have a predetermined range of possible answers which facilitate a quantification of the results. It is designed to answer such questions as how many or what proportion of the target population think or behave in this way or that, and what types of people within these populations stand out as being different from the norm.

However, a brief word should be said about qualitative research. Here the technique is not to use a structured questionnaire, but to set up more free-ranging interviews or, often, discussions among a group of peers – for example, analysts, employees or small shareholders. It is designed to generate ideas and insights into the way the target population thinks and behaves in relation to a wide range of topics, and provides an ideal input into the planning stage of a financial public relations programme or the development of a structured questionnaire.

Qualitative research is a particularly appropriate way of testing financial literature – annual reports and accounts, employee reports or financial advertising. It can identify how far these are likely to be read and understood, which messages are likely to be conveyed well or badly, the impact of visual style and layout, and the images these convey about the company.

Opinion research, whether it be qualitative or quantitative, is a natural complement to financial public relations. While research can define the problems – be they knowledge, attitude or behaviour – public relations must use the tools of the professional communicator to address them to achieve the desired ends.

13

Consultants or in-house: roles and relationships

Roger Hayes

The debate over in-house public relations staff versus consultancies and their relative merits will continue from one generation of management to the next as public relations evolves. It is by no means exclusive to financial public relations, but it does take on heightened significance in this sector, given both the priority placed upon it by top managements under pressure in a fast-changing and complex environment and the specialist technical expertise and broad strategic vision required.

That may seem to be hedging the bets. Specialist technical expertise is surely contradictory to broader strategic vision? The fact of the matter is, however, that experience on both sides of the fence leads to the definitive view that the public corporation should employ a mixture of in-house public relations executives and outside consultants.

Nowhere is this more true than in financial public relations, simply because of its technical nature and its crucial place in the corporate scheme of things.

Some corporations prefer to do it all themselves at enormous expense and without the necessary detachment consultants can bring to the boardroom table. Others (sometimes, but not always, for practical reasons) prefer to deal solely with consultants, treating them as the surrogate whipping boy without the internal sanctions and controls. This is logical for small companies unable to afford the luxury of in-house support staff other than the statutory company secretary.

Those organizations in the latter category, large or small, have the opportunity to develop a long-term relationship with a consultancy or pick one off the shelf for particular projects, discarding it thereafter, or both. There are a variety of cost/benefit calculations that can be made in this context from the point of view of the chief executive, always assuming of course that teams of different consultants are not scratching each others' eyes out in this competitive and still immature marketplace.

Alternatively, those corporations which keep everything to themselves lest outsiders contaminate the corporate culture or betray confidences tend to staff their public relations departments with complementary specialists, according to perceived priorities, one of which is certain to be financial public relations.

In practice, more corporations are recognizing that the optimum use of resources is a combination of the two.

Before discussing best practice and the ideal solution, it is important to reflect on the environment in which publicly quoted corporations – whether UK-based or multi-national, manufacturing or service, single product or diversified – find themselves. Traditionally, financial public relations, in-house or consultancy, has been UK-blinkered. Some still talk of 'City PR' and mean solely press relations – delivering the press release or the inspired leak to the City offices of the Sunday quality newspapers on Friday evening. Fortunately this approach is fast being overtaken, but not before time.

There are several clear reasons for this; there may well be more. Undoubtedly the most significant is the advent of shareholder sovereignty, particularly the investing institutions, which rightly or wrongly control most British corporations. The growth of international competition has forced corporations to devise strategies which have led to many takeovers and acquisitions. This has in turn led some enlightened corporations at least to communicate better with institutional fund managers and even with private shareholders, some of whom wear a different and important hat in that they also work there.

This has led more companies to realize that they can no longer rely solely on short and sweet annual general meetings, tacky annual reports and desultory media contact to reach the shareholder audience. They now also must use regular presentations, road shows, videos and carefully targeted publications.

To achieve a more enlightened approach to communication with shareholders and shareholder intermediaries (brokers/market makers/ analysts) needs more effective use of market research, tracking and profiling of shareholders. In addition, a more scientific understanding of the interrelationships between institutional and private shareholders, intermediaries and the media is needed.

Information technology has eased the problems of identification, tracking and analysis, but it has in its wake led to far greater investor access to global markets and to far speedier response. Deregulation of financial markets, either pre-empting or responding to this trend, has aggravated the scale of the problem or opportunity, depending on knowledge of, and ability to interrogate, databases.

Further trends have arisen from these explosive developments, namely the boom in communication which has followed the financial community's own Big Bang.

The changing relationships and interdependencies between corporations and their suppliers, customers, competitors, employees and regulatory bodies, both in the UK and transnationally, has not only made it even more imperative that financial public relations executives and consultants understand these dynamics in order to respond to them, but has complicated the interpretation of financial data. More creative ways have been found by corporate treasurers and accountants to manage cash flow and earnings per share, and non-financial as well as financial expertise is more than ever required to make public relations judgements and decisions. For instance, those people fortunate enough to have legal, political, strategic planning, human resource and marketing backgrounds, in addition to possessing research, computer and of course financial experience, have a distinct advantage in the financial public relations field.

There are three (at least) conclusions from these trends, which have put credibility and consistent communication to a wider, overlapping group of stakeholders at centre stage. It is obvious from the above analysis that no individual will possess all the requisite skills. But they are all needed by corporations.

Firstly, there is the need for an executive who is capable of advising the corporation on the communication implications of these trends and managing the implementation. That person must be strategic and broad.

Secondly, there is a need for specialists in all the disciplines referred to, for making up the financial public relations or, as it is now often called, investor relations team. These people can either be in-house or external consultants.

In addition, corporations require from their consultants a mix of executives capable of developing long-term relationships with the client, so as to know enough about the organization to be accepted within and to be able to act on behalf of the client with brokers, fund managers and the media. There is also a need for consultants who have particular areas of expertise – in the new issue, privatization or takeover fields to cite three examples – whose skills can be tapped as required.

It is difficult to be precise about what is the most desirable. There are as many different solutions in this fragmented business as there are companies, and all the variations are, at different times, required. This is such an embryonic business that it will be many years (if ever) before any definitive hypothesis can be satisfactorily tested.

Best practice so far indicates that of those companies which treat financial public relations seriously (far too few but an increasing number, often after the horse has bolted) the vast majority have an in-house specialist but use outside help at a strategic or specialist or project level, or at all three. It is partly a matter of resources, but also the style of the chairman or chief executive. If he or she treats it seriously, then investor relations will take its place in the executive suite. This is an essential precondition of a successful use of consultants, certainly in the larger corporations.

There is still the constraint of the battles for position between company secretary, finance department and public relations, in which the last traditionally has not had much clout. Where a senior in-house investor relations person or outside specialist has the stature and credibility, conflicts can soon be resolved. Fortunately financial public relations is responding to these developments by increasingly bringing on board those with the different skills required for a successful investor relations programme.

In addition to having a good relationship with the chief executive and finance director, the outside consultant usually finds it helps to have a peer in-house who understands his field and his demands and is able to meet various pressures and deadlines. If this in-house person is also a specialist in investor relations, so much the better, because he or she will have the necessary ability and antennae to find the way around the corporate maze and through the minefields. Few consultants, except in rare circumstances, can possibly have the same insight or knowledge of the dynamics of particular corporations as in-house professionals, especially if they sit on the major committees where the decisions take place.

It is the in-house executive who has the necessary access to the company secretary, the chief accountant, the treasurer and so on on a day-to-day basis, so as to be able to deal directly with the media, brokers and fund managers as a spokesperson, as well as provide outside consultants with relevant facts and figures so they can do their job. But both in-house professionals and consultants can have equal access to the corporation's bankers, lawyers, brokers and auditors, and that is how it should be.

There is always so much effort required to untangle the shareholder register, answer all manner of enquiries, write the annual report copy and sort out who should be invited to which presentation, that the combined resources of both the outside consultant and the in-house team are usually necessary.

Ideally, the consultant should sit on an investor relations committee, along with other advisers, chaired by a director (preferably the chief executive to show commitment), with the in-house public relations executive as secretary. This is often done in the public affairs/policy field but seldom in investor relations, which is odd in view of its importance. At least acting as secretary gives the financial public relations officer control of the agenda as a trade-off from the chore of writing the minutes.

Many in-house public relations departments, saddled with all the daily detail of lists, invitations, progressing projects, answering telephone enquiries and writing texts, rail against the supposed lack of involvement on the part of the consultant, who tends to have the juicier strategic tasks. A healthy (sometimes unhealthy) tension, which is often unjustified, sets in unless the consultant is long on promise and short on delivery.

The reality is that this division of labour is the best use of in-house and consultancy time. The added value the consultant should bring to the table is the fact that he or she is dealing with the same outside contacts for a variety of clients, studies the changing face of financial markets, undertakes research with greater detachment, can advise on the changing relationship between shareholder, analyst, market maker and journalist, and, above all, can spend time on creative thinking and bounce ideas off harassed internal executives.

As a generalization, the biggest constraint still is the lack of comprehension by top management of the need for skilful and sustained financial public relations, which is aggravated by the patchy nature of advice and implementation. Over-promising is still rampant, adding to the credibility gap as expectations are raised by the narrow definition of investor relations still offered by too many practitioners, many of whom also do not speak the language of management.

So best practice is not solely about an optimum use of internal and external resources – both are required – but about overcoming the limitations on investor relations development brought about by lack of specialist knowledge, fragmentation, and insufficient people with the clout to integrate investor relations into the broader corporate communication picture and management decision-making process.

Case study 1

London's biggest private issue: the flotation of the Wellcome Foundation

Wellcome PLC is one of Europe's major pharmaceutical companies, with a market capitalization at the time of writing (March 1988) of more than £4bn. In its financial year to end August 1987 Wellcome's pre-tax profits amounted to £169m.

The company's origins go back to 1880 when Burroughs Wellcome & Co. was founded by two young American pharmacists, Henry Wellcome and Silas Burroughs. The US subsidiary of the company is still known as Burroughs Wellcome Co. Under the will of the late Sir Henry Wellcome, who died in 1936, a trust was set up, The Wellcome Trust, which, before the flotation in 1986 of part of the equity of Wellcome, owned 100 per cent of the company.

The chairman of the board of trustees, Sir David Steel, announcing the intention to sell approximately 20 per cent of its shareholding in Wellcome, commented:

> The trustees have for some time been concerned about the wisdom of having all their eggs in one basket, notwithstanding the excellence of that basket. They have taken professional advice and have now decided on this course of action. This will enable the trust to diversify its investments and increase its aid to medical research at a time when funds are badly needed. At the same time the integrity and independence of the foundation will be preserved and the close links between the trust and the foundation will be maintained.

This case study tells of the story of the flotation of Wellcome and the role played by the investor relations division of Valin Pollen (now Carter Valin Pollen), the financial public relations and investor relations consultancy, which was selected for the largest flotation of a private company on the London stock market (if the special case of TSB is excluded).

There were five primary target audiences addressed during the run-up to the flotation. They were institutional investors, pharmaceuticals analysts, the financial and business press, private investors, and employees in their roles as members of staff and also potential investors.

The major problem as far as institutions, analysts and the press were concerned was almost complete lack of awareness of Wellcome and much confusion between The Wellcome Foundation, the company, and The Wellcome Trust, the sole shareholder. The Wellcome Foundation differed from most of its competitors in the pharmaceutical industry in the spread of its therapeutic portfolio. Several commentators, both among the analyst community and in the press, put forward the notion that this wide spread of products was due to the fact that Wellcome was academically rather than commercially focused, in part fuelled by the trust owning the company and the academic research sponsorship activities of the trust. This turned out to be a deeply entrenched attitude emerging in the benchmark research study referred to later; although it was to be changed significantly during the run up to the flotation, from time to time it resurfaced as an issue.

The other major difficulty with the Wellcome Foundation was comparability. Its peers in the UK included ICI, Glaxo, Beecham and Fisons. The pharmaceutical side of ICI was, however, only a division within the company; Beecham had extensive operations beyond pharmaceuticals; Fisons had only recently stripped away its fertilizer production activities and its range of drugs was relatively limited; and this left Glaxo as the most appropriate comparison. This was unfortunate to some degree in that Glaxo had – and still has – what is known in the industry as a 'blockbuster' in its product range with its anti-ulcer Zantac, the only drug then existing to compete with Tagamet, which had been developed by Sir James Black at Smith, Kline & French.

Certain senior personnel left the company around the lead-up to flotation. Any fears concerning this were soon dispelled when it was realized that the company had management strength in depth and the gaps were quickly and satisfactorily plugged.

When the Wellcome management team made its final presentation to institutional investors before impact day, the line-up included the chairman, Alfred Shepperd, and the finance director, Martin Brookman. Other members of the team included Dr Ronald Cresswell, research director, the new US chief executive, Ted Haigler, and his vice-president, marketing and sales, Peter Reckert.

In order to define the issues facing Wellcome among the financial community and to assess levels of awareness of the company, its therapeutic portfolio, its financial performance and its strengths and weaknesses, Valin Pollen commissioned Consensus Research to undertake a major City research study addressing these questions. The study came up with the following main findings:

1   The general response to the flotation was favourable, owing to a shortage of companies in the pharmaceuticals sector.
2   Both analysts and fund managers knew little about Wellcome.
3   Where knowledge did exist, the company was seen to have many strengths by those who knew it, particularly its research base, its wide product range, its focus on ethical drugs and its link with the excellent reputation of The Wellcome Trust.
4   However, it was perceived to have a number of weaknesses, including its vaccine market, which was seen as declining; its lack of commercialism; its commitment to the Third World and its dependence on the dollar. Paradoxically, its range of products was seen by some as being too wide.

In fact, Wellcome was, and is, a highly efficient and marketing-orientated company with strong management and a drugs portfolio of substantial potential.

On the basis of this study, a planned communication programme was set in motion and continued through impact day and the trading of Wellcome shares on the Stock Exchange.

It was clear from the initial results that a higher profile communication programme was required and significant time would have to be spent educating the investment community on the fundamental strengths of Wellcome. The following marketing and communication strategy was recommended and agreed:

- Rapidly raising awareness of the company and its range of products.
- Correcting misperceptions, particularly those concerning the commercialism of the company's management and its research focus.
- Encouraging interest among high-net-worth private individuals in order to create a degree of competition for the stock between those investors and the institutions.

It was clear from the outset that a careful and controlled build-up of awareness in Wellcome would be necessary. As it turned out, a great deal of education was required in the pharmaceuticals industry itself.

Senior financial correspondents, including City editors, and pharmaceuticals industry correspondents were introduced to the company on a one-to-one basis and given careful initial briefings. When lines of communication had been opened up with the company, journalists were encouraged to use them.

A core group of analysts was identified and introduced to the company. In addition, groups of analysts were taken round the pharmaceuticals production plant at Dartford and the company's research laboratories at Beckenham. A trip to Research Triangle Park, the headquarters of the US operations of Burroughs Wellcome, was also organized for analysts.

Build-up continued towards the major institutional presentations and, as part of the process, a corporate video on Wellcome was produced. Explanatory booklets were prepared for the staff, with an employee video explaining the mechanics of the flotation and how employees could go about applying for shares. Despite the unsatisfactory way in which the news of the flotation broke – a press leak – employee communication was managed professionally and carefully and there was little negative feedback.

The major constraint as far as the marketing programme was concerned turned out not to be difficulties in understanding Wellcome but comparability with Glaxo. Pricing was an extremely difficult issue.

Given the careful build-up, the marketing team felt sure that the demand for Wellcome stock would be heavy and that it should be priced accordingly. However, it was also recognized that a possible ceiling on the Wellcome price could be the multiple enjoyed by Glaxo, as Wellcome did not have a blockbuster drug like Zantac in its portfolio. Wellcome had broken through in the area of anti-virals with its anti-herpes drug Zovirax, but Retrovir, the anti-AIDS drug, was still to come.

However, the pre-flotation research results were very encouraging. The initial benchmark study among institutions, analysts and financial journalists was replicated in December 1985, six months after the start of the communication programme. The key findings were as follows:

1 The proportion of the sample rating the health sector as 'very attractive' had risen from 29 per cent to 39 per cent.
2 Since the July study Wellcome's image had strengthened in most of the key image attributes measured, including the strength of its management (an uplift of 22 percentage points), its attractiveness on short-term and long-term investment opportunities (+5 points and +6 points), the soundness of its financial record (+12 points) and – not surprisingly given its efforts – its communication with the City (+8 points).
3 Awareness of Wellcome's flotation on a *spontaneous* basis had increased from 11 per cent to 47 per cent, similar to some of the then current privatization issues, including TSB (41 per cent) and British Airways (46 per cent).

4   The results of the active press programme vindicated the huge efforts in this area, as Table CS1.1 on how respondents' attention was drawn to Wellcome demonstrates.

Table CS1.1

BASE: 70	*July 1985(%)*	*December 1985(%)*
Press comment	14	77
Seen advertising	29	59
Received documentation	14	40
Read brokers' circulars	26	40

While the communication strategy was coming through in terms of the City, two concerns remained:

(a) An increased proportion of the sample qualified their interest in investing in Wellcome by saying that it depended on the price (an uplift of 7 percentage points); and this, with the greater long-term investment attractiveness of Glaxo at that time (Wellcome scored 77 per cent, Glaxo 84 per cent), suggested a final marketing push was required.
(b) The company and its financial advisers had been reluctant to market the issue to private investors and the element of competition for the stock was missing.

Consequently, it was decided to increase direct communication with the press to build on success in this area and run a short high-profile corporate advertising programme aimed at encouraging high-net-worth individuals to take an interest in the company.

The advertising spend was relatively modest (about £500,000) but the campaign was carefully targeted and the results were dramatic. Prospectus applications flooded the merchant bankers to the issue, Robert Fleming & Co.

A survey of private client brokers showed 87 per cent said their clients were interested in investing in Wellcome, and 65 per cent said they were likely to advise their clients to invest in the issue. The outcome was neatly summarized by the Tempus column of *The Times*: 'What a welcome for Wellcome!'.

The shares were offered at 120p and the issue – to raise £250m – was seventeen times oversubscribed. Around 430,000 applicants (then the largest and possibly still the largest number of applications received for a non-privatization issue) applied for 3,750m shares as against the 210.8m on offer – and the shares opened on a 40p premium on the first day of trading.

Case study 2

A watershed in takeover defence – Siebe's bid for APV

At the beginning of 1988, APV announced a major reorganization of the group and the launch of a new corporate identity to be implemented world-wide. This followed the acquisition during 1987 of Baker Perkins and Pasilac, which established the enlarged group as the world leader in the manufacture of process engineering for the food and beverage industries.

The new APV is the culmination of a long-term strategy developed by its chief executive, Fred Smith. However, his plans almost came to an abrupt halt in 1986 when Siebe, an acquisitive conglomerate, launched a surprise £182m bid for APV. It seemed perfect timing. Fred Smith had begun the process of reorganizing the old APV, but his efforts had not had time to have a significant effect on the bottom line, or to be recognized by the Stock Market.

The reaction of the City to Siebe's bid seemed conclusive. The market response varied from 'generous' to 'knockout'. Siebe's chief executive, Barry Stephens, himself described the proposed takeover as 'a magical marriage', a phrase picked up by a number of journalists. Some investment analysts were quoted as saying the offer was too good to refuse or at the very least that it would be a very tough battle to fight.

It was against this background that the APV chairman, Sir Ronald McIntosh, and chief executive, Fred Smith, gathered with their advisers S. G. Warburg to consider their defence strategy. APV had no public relations or investor relations consultancy, so, after talking to a number of agencies, it appointed Valin Pollen. It took two months of intense and unrelenting activity to defeat the bid from Siebe.

There were a number of procedures which had to be instituted as soon as possible. Events move very fast during a takeover. Many parties are working on different aspects of the defence and all need to be informed. Checklists of names, telephone numbers and fax numbers were assembled. All the investment analysts and journalists who might be expected to be interested in the takeover were identified. All advisers were given a thorough briefing about APV and began to gather as much information as possible about the opposition.

Before the framework was in place, a programme of meetings with key analysts and journalists was started. There were then strict guidelines about the level of contact allowed during a takeover and meetings were limited to individuals, one at a time. A stream of analysts and press was invited to APV's headquarters in Crawley, where they were given a tour of the site followed by the opportunity to question senior directors. For others who could not manage the trip, interviews were arranged in London.

The process was time-consuming but invaluable. APV had an unenviably low profile in the City and the base of knowledge had to be raised quickly. Once established, the contact was sustained with frequent telephone calls to provide updates, to ascertain whether press reports or brokers' circulars were going to appear, and to identify what contact members of the target audience had with the other side.

It is crucial to win the goodwill of commentators early on and to ensure that what they write will be against an informed background and an accurate knowledge of the group. The success of this exercise was due mainly to the energy and enthusiasm of the chairman and chief executive and to the convincing case they argued for staying independent.

An area where APV was not lacking in contact was with its own institutional shareholders. Chairman Sir Ronald McIntosh maintained contact with APV's major shareholders and was able to limit any significant selling in the market, asking investors to wait before making a decision until APV was able to publish its defence document and argue its position thoroughly. Goodwill is only half the battle, however. Several people expressed the sentiment that it was a pity the bid had been made and that APV's management appeared to be on an upward trend. But Siebe too was impressive, and the offer did indeed seem attractive.

It quickly became clear that four needs had to be addressed. Firstly, a profits forecast for 1986. Secondly, some impressive and convincing market information to indicate that strong profits growth would continue in 1987 and 1988 and beyond. Thirdly, any information which would weaken the opposition's arguments that there was a clear industrial logic for the merger and that Siebe's management would perform a faster and better job than APV's existing management. Fourthly, moves to foster and encourage the widening sentiment among fund managers that they had a duty to support an incumbent management if it had been seen to be doing a good job.

Some investment analysts had been quoted as saying that the offer was generous. APV was respected by the engineering community but the general consensus was that the opening price, which put the prospective price/earnings ratio at around 18, seemed very attractive. APV had only recently announced its preliminary results of £17m pre-tax, and the average forecast for the current year was around £19m to £21m.

It was agreed early on that the profits forecast could and should be made. The question was, how soon could the auditors complete the exercise and when, tactically, would it be the most effective time to publish it? The uncertainty helped APV's cause, but care had to be taken not to let the market run away with over-ambitious guesses at what the forecast would be.

It took a careful and patient reiteration of a series of arguments to gain market confidence in APV's growth potential without of course making a profits forecast – which was anyway, at that stage, unknown. Siebe had made an offer of convertible preference shares, which the press had described as 'funny money', only being convertible into ordinary shares from 1988. Shareholders seemed to agree, as there was little selling of APV shares. The more time passed, the stronger APV's case became and the more likely it seemed that Siebe would have to offer cash to win.

APV's annual meeting was scheduled for 23 May and there was some debate about whether to issue the defence document on that day or aim to have two bites of the cherry by sending the chairman's statement to shareholders, following up with the defence document later.

Sir Ronald McIntosh decided to take the opportunity of the AGM to speak directly to his shareholders in a statement which allowed his personal style to come through more strongly than would be possible through the formal defence document. The statement was printed and sent to shareholders and read out at the AGM. He suggested, for example, that 'It would be best if the directors of Siebe stuck to protective clothing and garages, with which they are familiar, and left us to get on with the specialized process engineering which is APV's business'. He went on to say that 'the only synergy that I can think of between our two businesses is if someone wanted to build an underwater dairy, using our process plant and Siebe's breathing apparatus. The demands for such a project would probably be limited'.

He reminded shareholders that 1986 was Industry Year and asked 'What relevance do opportunist acquisitions, financed by fancy paper, have to the process of wealth creation?'. This theme was to become of increasing importance as the bid proceeded.

The defence document was published six days later. It argued convincingly the strength and depth of APV's management and the particular skills that are required in the specialized area of process engineering. It countered Siebe's claim that there was an industrial logic and fit between the two companies. It also made a number of assertions about Siebe's financial and management record.

It was the beginning of a 'gloves-off' approach from APV. The constraints of the Takeover Code meant that the wording was tentative, but it hit home sufficiently to rattle the opposition. To take one example: 'Questions are being asked about the extent to which Siebe's apparent profit growth is based on the creative use of acquisition accounting . . . How much have past results benefitted from provisions made against the assets of previous acquisitions?'

Siebe replied to APV's defence document on 6 June by announcing that it was making an increased final offer, based on an assumption that APV would make a pre-tax profits forecast of £26m. It also introduced a cash alternative.

The APV camp was taken by surprise with this announcement. It was most unusual to make a final offer *before* the profits forecast was known.

APV came out with its profits forecast on 11 June at £27m, including £0.9m profit from sales of property. This brought down the exit P/E on the cash alternative to an acceptable 12.8 times APV's forecast earnings, compared with the historic average multiple of 15.6 times for the FT Actuaries Industrial Group.

Siebe issued its official offer document on 13 June and was clearly disturbed by the questions on accounting issues. It published a comprehensive letter from its auditors responding to these questions.

Sir Ronald McIntosh was not pleased with the inclusion of this letter in Siebe's document and responded by writing to shareholders a few days later saying that he had posed thirteen questions concerning Siebe's preliminary announcements of results, the majority of which remained unanswered. He described the auditors' letter as 'convoluted' but said that, where it did respond clearly to APV's questions, it only confirmed their suspicions about Siebe's results. APV felt that it had been particularly unfair for Siebe to bring forward the publication of its preliminary results by approximately seven weeks in an attempt to influence the outcome of the bid, yet refused to publish its full accounts before the final closing date. APV argued that the report and accounts were essential to a proper evaluation of the proposals.

With the deadline of the final closing date approaching, it was time for APV to return to its major shareholders and give them a last convincing argument. A short presentation, supported with visual aids, was prepared, and the chairman and chief executive took it on a tour of a number of institutions. Their case won a sympathetic hearing. Finally, the closing date for accepting Siebe's offer arrived. Siebe and its associate, Kleinwort Benson, who already held a total of 27.5 per cent of APV and had received 0.8 per cent acceptances, won only a further 5.9 per cent acceptances, taking their total holding to 34.2 per cent.

The battle was over. APV had won.

The bid proved to be something of a turning point, removing the bias that had tended to be shown in favour of predators. There had been increasing disquiet over the recent spate of takeovers in which conglomerates had acquired good specialist companies. After the APV–Siebe battle, victory for the predator was no longer seen as an almost inevitable conclusion.

Case study 3

Balancing a company's share register

Neil Ryder

Today BET is described as 'the international services company'. It is the idea that one company can provide an integrated range of support services to industrial, commercial and public sector customers all over the world which has provided the momentum throughout a restructuring phase which took some five years. The changes have taken the company from one which was seen as a potential takeover target back in 1982 with a market value of only £240m to one which in 1988 is worth nearly £2bn (even after the market crash of 1987) and which turns over £2bn a year.

BET has been totally transformed and, far from being the investment trust it used to be, it now has an identity of its own. It has defined its mission in life, which is to be the world leader in support services; it has sold companies which did not fit with the core support services strategy; and it has bought others which have helped it to consolidate its position as leader in each of the markets in which it operates.

It was the scale of change both in the size of the business and in the nature of the business which made the company concentrate on developing ways in which it could communicate its strategy to its shareholders and solicit their support in backing BET throughout the process of change. It has included about 200 acquisitions, forty disposals and an increase in share capital of eight times the 1982 figure.

The process took time, and underlying it there was one fundamental factor: the overriding need to look at the business in the long-term, not the short- to medium-term. The task was to reorientate the business away from the label 'conglomerate', with its implications of limited life, towards a new breed of service business being built for the long-term future.

Contrary to popular belief perhaps, the City is not preoccupied with looking only at the short-term issues. As long as the City understands what it is that you want to achieve five or ten years from now, then it will be prepared to support you wholeheartedly, even though it may complain a little when earnings growth takes some temporary punishment in the process.

Because we were taking a long-term view, we wanted to identify those existing and potential shareholders who were likely to take a long-term view too, and stick with us throughout the changes. The first task therefore was to look at our share register to see who was on it.

Firstly, we found that there was a surprising preponderance of private investors. Including those individuals using nominee names, more than 30 per cent of shareholders were private individuals. That was good news because private shareholders also usually take a longer-term view of an investment than the more active institutions. Secondly, and not surprisingly, we found that a good many institutions were missing – institutions that we felt should be there. The question was, why were they not there? Thirdly, among the other institutions which held BET stock, it was obvious that BET was not being treated as a core investment.

Faced with that situation, we decided that the only way to shift the balance of our shareholder register was to research the UK equity market. Initially, we drew up lists of the top insurance companies, pension funds, investment trusts, unit trusts, banks and the like, and collected data on how much money each of them had invested in UK equities and what proportion of the total UK equity market that represented.

So, for example, if a particular pension fund owns 6 per cent or 7 per cent of all UK market shares, then it would seem reasonable, though simplistic, to assume that it might own 6 per cent or 7 per cent of BET shares. If it only owned 1 per cent, then we would consider it underweight in our shares and we would obviously have to find out why.

Then we researched the shareholder registers of other companies so that we could identify those investors who shared common investment characteristics. For instance, we noticed a pattern in the institutional investors who held few shares in companies which had interests in South Africa, and we identified those investors who appeared to like stocks with a fairly high yield as opposed to high growth.

Finally, we researched City attitudes to BET to find out what perceptions of the company were among the investment community. We have continued to do that once a year ever since so we can identify how far we are succeeding in changing the view of BET from conglomerate to services company.

That data allowed us to put together a fairly detailed marketing plan, which comprised three simple lists. List A pulled together those institutions which were extremely underweight in our shares. List B represented the institutions which were overweight in our shares, and obviously we wanted them to stay that way. List C had on it those institutions which were not grossly underweight but which we felt could do with some topping up.

At the same time we developed a computer system – called the share dealing system – which we used to monitor and log our progress. The development of that system was important because every piece of information, no matter how seemingly trivial, was helpful in putting together a complete picture of the balance in our shareholder register.

Having targeted the audiences, the next question to ask was 'What are we going to do now?' There are many thousands of pension funds in the UK alone, so it would have been impossible to give each of them a separate presentation. We needed a wholesaler, someone who could be an effective catalyst and who could be trusted to help us meet the A and B list people on a regular basis and who would pass the message on down to list C and beyond. So attention turned to the brokers.

Again research played an important part. In looking at the broker population we identified just how comprehensive, frequent and accurate each of the analysts were in their reports on us. We investigated each broker's volume of trade in our shares and entered it on our computer system, which meant that we could monitor trading volume by broker and identify any patterns which emerged.

In our research in the City we added a question for fund managers – 'Which analysts do you trust the most?' A bit unconventional maybe, but it worked, and we backed up our findings with findings from other independent surveys of analysts which rate the performance of each of them, sector by sector.

By that time we had a fairly good picture of who constituted the top brokers, the credibility of the analysts and their ability to understand and deal in BET stock. With that information we drew up two lists. The top six analysts in our sector – industrial holding companies – were put on list A. The second tier six analysts were put on list B.

At that stage advisers also came into the equation and needed to be researched. For example, if we identified Cambridge County Council pension fund as an A list candidate and then found that its portfolio was managed by someone else, say Warburg Asset Management, then that adviser must, by definition, go on the A list too.

With the information in place we then began to do something practical about shifting the balance of the shareholder register. We formalized the programme of meeting A and B list analysts and developed proper channels of communication. Then, after a short period, we found that even though some of the analysts were fairly bullish about BET, that positive attitude was not reflected in the trading levels of their particular houses.

We discovered that the break in the chain between analysts and investors was the brokers' sales teams, none of which had any form of direct connection or communication with BET. They were our next target audience, and over three years we have presented regularly to the sales teams so we can actually get at those who are at the sharp end of the deal.

One of the major benefits of targeting which institutions on A and B lists are worth pursuing, and which brokers they use, was that we were able to control who came to what presentation. Large groups of institutions, up to, say, twenty people, were arranged through the relevant analyst, and he or she invited people from lists A, B and C. The important distinction, though, was that we told the analyst exactly whom to invite, avoiding the embarrassment, for both us and the broker concerned, of one fund manager being invited by several different brokers. After the presentations a full record of the meeting was entered on to the share dealing system, including details of who spoke to whom, when, where and what about.

We also reviewed our other communication channels. We improved our annual report and took a fresh, and novel, look at takeover documents after realizing just how confusing and incomprehensible they were. We even did battle with the banks and the lawyers, who always seemed to substitute confusion for communication. Nothing has changed; we are still fighting them. They still will not accept that when we say we are going to have the Paris listing presentation up the Eiffel Tower, or the Amsterdam listing presentation in an old building with no electricity in the ancient part of the city, we mean it. Contrary to popular belief, investors like work to be fun too!

Of course one has to be flexible because some funds have different policies. Some do not like meeting privately at all, while others go to the opposite extreme and like to meet us regularly. The Norwich Union, one of our largest shareholders, likes one meeting a year and expects it to be comprehensive in scope.

So far our approach seems to be working. The balance of our register has both shifted and become more stable. We have increased the number of shares held by people on the A and C lists and we have kept loyal to those on our B list. We have enlarged the number of private shareholders considerably, not only in the UK but also overseas.

Throughout this period of intense and highly visible activity in the UK we were active behind the scenes in preparing for overseas listings in Europe and in North America. Before listing in the US, we spent two years educating retail brokers there about BET by visiting them in any corner of the country we could find them. We were convinced that we could not rely just on a roadshow to achieve a wider shareholder base among private investors. For us there was no substitute for visiting the retail brokerages, particularly in areas where we had existing operations, and leaving with a commitment to come back regularly and tell them how things are going.

It paid off: 65 per cent of the $100m worth of American depository receipts we issued went to private investors and our ADRs fared much better than most in the October 1987 crash in overseas ownership.

Alongside our commitment to meeting with A and B list people, we have put a good deal of effort into widening our private shareholder base in the UK. The BET Experience is a twice-yearly, regionally based event, aimed at keeping all our private investors loyal to BET.

The programme allows every one of our shareholders to visit a BET Experience at least once every five years. They can bring a guest along with them too, which helps to enlarge our private investor population.

We try to make the evening as informative and as entertaining as we can. There are quizzes to enter, prizes to be won (all provided by BET companies) and a good time is usually had by all, including our staff, who say that the BET Experience makes an important contribution to employee motivation and customer marketing too.

The whole programme depends on the commitment and goodwill of senior and operating management, but also on the research and planning that are essential to any marketing programme.

Case study 4

A new identity for Akzo

John Smythe

The chemical company Akzo launched its new corporate identity to the world in March 1988. Why did Akzo need a new identity? A look at its history indicates one of the reasons: Akzo is composed of hundreds of different companies, not all having the same name.

Akzo is one of the world's major chemical companies, operating in all sectors, from chemicals, through fibres and coatings, to healthcare products. The company has more than 250 operating units in 50 countries. It has nearly 70,000 employees and turned over approximately $8bn in 1987.

Perhaps surprisingly, Akzo is less than 20 years old – young by most standards in the chemical industry. However, its roots go back as far as the late eighteenth century. Some of the well known company and brand names belonging to the group are Sikkens (paints), Enka (fibres) and Organon (pharmaceuticals).

By the 1960s those hundreds of companies had amalgamated to form two conglomerates – Vereinigte Glanzstoff Fabriken (VGF) and Algemene Kunstzijde Unie (AKU). Early in 1969 AKU and VGF united, one of the first Dutch-German mergers. The company made man-made fibres for domestic, household and industrial applications.

Another big chemicals group, Koninklijke Zout Organon (KZO), merged with the new company later that year, with the aim of reducing AKU's product spread and of making KZO's operations much more international in nature. AK(U) and (K)ZO made AKZO!

By 1985 Akzo was a disparate group of organizations with different names, different backgrounds and different management methods. Because of this, it was run as a set of more or less autonomous divisions. Notwithstanding the decentralized approach, Akzo was able to grow to be the fifteenth largest chemical company in the world. On the way, however, it had to weather a number of storms, such as a huge over-capacity in the production of fibres in Europe and a general world recession exacerbated by the oil crisis.

Between 1982 and 1985 the group recovered, and the various divisions and operating units acquired excellent reputations (and product lines) – but only in their own countries and own markets. It was apparent to the board of management that Akzo itself – the corporation – was unknown outside Holland. Indeed in West Germany it was mostly known as Enka. The competition, on the other hand, had much better developed images. It was clear that what had been right for Akzo in the 1970s – an autonomous organizational structure – was no longer suitable.

So the Akzo top management looked at Akzo's goals and strategies, and produced the Akzo Mission Statement, a vehicle by which the organization's corporate vision was projected. Basically it said that Akzo's primary strengths as an organization lay in the flexibility and innovation it brought to all business dealings. The new business plan focused on three product areas:

- Basic industrial.
- Technology-based.
- High growth/high risk.

The weak points of the company were also analyzed, and it was decided to pay special attention to the three most important aspects:

- corporate identity
- human resources
- research and development

UK corporate identity consultancy Wolff Olins was appointed in 1986 to create a new identity for Akzo. According to Wolff Olins, it is impossible merely to design a new letterhead for a complex organization like Akzo and say 'There is your new identity'. One has to have a very clear idea of what the company does – what it makes and sells, what its personnel's behaviour is like, what the outside world thinks of the company and so on – and one has to examine existing strategies for their validity before recommending a new identity.

The first stage began with a thorough investigation into what Akzo was like, and how it differed from the competition; for, given that Akzo was very much like the competition in terms of *quantifiable* characteristics, it was the intangible differences – its reputation, for example – which would help Akzo compete successfully, and become better known, and which had to be reflected in the identity.

The prime objective was to draw a clear picture of how different groups of people perceived Akzo and its many parts and from that to define the corporate characteristics the company currently had. The investigation confirmed Akzo's feelings that its true achievements were not well known and that its profile was not as well developed as those of the competition.

There was a lot of confusion about what people thought Akzo did. Some people were familiar with some of its activities; very few knew about everything that it did. Some of the operating companies, such as Enka, Sikkens and Organon, were familiar names, but they were not associated with Akzo. One journalist knew all three names and more or less what each company did, but he was astonished to discover that they were in any way related.

The positive findings were that Akzo was:

- Flexible.
- Innovative.
- Entrepreneurial.
- Responsive.
- Prudent.
- Decentralized.
- Accountable.

At the same time, Akzo was becoming:

- Established in the marketplace.
- Confident.
- Global in scope.
- Strong.
- One company with a balanced product mix.

The message could be crystallized in the phrase 'diversity within unity', with the individual working within a large organization perceived as the key to success. The working theme for the designers became 'achievement and the individual'.

Any corporate identity has two parts: name structure and style. Name structure affects the way an organization presents its operations. Akzo's new identity has had a number of repercussions on its names. In the past, names used included the corporate Akzo name, divisional names, (including Enka), operating company and business unit names and country organization names. Some of these have been, or will be, changed.

Akzo is still called Akzo. However, the system by which its various parts have been named in the past has been rationalized. Most, but not all, Akzo operations had Akzo in their names; some used their divisional names world-wide; others only used them internally, preferring to use a different name in the marketplace.

The new system makes sense internationally (previously, divisional names were Dutch throughout the world), and accommodates the complex series of markets in which Akzo operates. So within Akzo there are now examples of three types of identity: monolithic, endorsed and branded. There is a simple rule governing nomenclature which states that the more industrial the market a particular operating unit is in, the more Akzo everything should be. Hence the Akzo identity is presented to the outside world by every division, with the division's activity indicated in the language of the country in which it is active.

As to style, what should the identity look like? Akzo had to consider the advantages and disadvantages of either keeping its existing 'triangle' identity, using a 'tile' system like Enka's, or conceiving a completely new identity.

It was agreed that a completely new symbol would be developed. All the other large chemical companies have typographical identities which have a familiarity and power because they have been around a long time, not from any intrinsic strength. So it was decided to use a totally different kind of visual approach – because Akzo *is* different.

Firstly, the name: a new way of writing the word Akzo when linked to the symbol was developed. Secondly, the symbol: the obvious chemicals-based routes were considered first, for example alchemy and the four humours. However, it soon became apparent that that was suitable for small companies but not large industrial conglomerates.

It was while considering a figurative scheme for Akzo based on natural order that the basis of the new symbol was discovered: a bas relief of human form with arms outstretched. Originally a figurehead outside a place of education in Greece, the sculpture had been used by students as a measurement tool – the span of the arms was a unit of length and the body as a whole was believed to be in perfect proportion. So the figure was both a scientific and an artistic symbol. See Figure CS4.1.

A number of approaches were explored before the final version of the symbol was reached; they included graphic techniques such as etching and linocut, and computer generation, but in the end the best solution, and the simplest, was actually to draw the symbol. It appears neither dressed nor naked (for socio-cultural reasons it would not have been appropriate naked). The symbol is thus not masculine, rather it is human – mankind striving and achieving.

The new symbol was tested by the Institute for Psychological Market Research, which talked to both Akzo personnel and the general public. The verdict was that the new symbol was preferable to the old triangle. Most said that it evoked associations which matched the desired image of Akzo. In particular, it was felt to say 'worldwide, wide-ranging, future-orientated and strong'.

Simply producing the new symbol and making the name changes were

Figure CS4.1   *For the Dutch chemicals giant, Akzo, a new corporate symbol was based on a Greek statue, and combined strongly with the brief name (created by Wolff Olins)*

obviously not enough. They had to be communicated, and communicated convincingly and dramatically. That required a mental change, an acceptance and a commitment to the new Akzo. If your personnel are not on your side, the new identity will languish in a cupboard.

Akzo therefore devised a long-term internal and external communication programme. Internally this began in December 1987 with a two-day senior management conference. It was supplemented by videos, laser machines, dramatic music and multi-projector slide presentations, run like a military machine, and told 300 top Akzo managers from all over the world (day one) and 100 public relations personnel (day two) just why Akzo needed a new corporate identity, how it had been devised and how it would be communicated and implemented.

Each day opened with an introduction by the presenter – Angela Rippon, the television personality and broadcaster – who was specially flown in for the period. The programmes included presentations by top executives and the showing of a film on Akzo's position in the industry. See Figure CS4.2.

Each day culminated in the unveiling of an illuminated sign destined for an Akzo office block, cocktails, dinner and an international cabaret. Akzo even had a song specially composed for the occasion, on the subject of the new symbol!

Figure CS4.2 *To launch its new identity Akzo staged a historical exhibition (created by Wolff Olins)*

The communication programme continued throughout the early part of 1988. Its culmination was the official launch on the publication of the 1987 annual report on 31 March 1988.

Akzo's five divisions held presentations similar to those given in December for their own top management, the people who would pass on the message lower down the line. The UK and US operations, both of them significant to Akzo in terms of turnover and future activities, were also informed, via presentations in London and New York.

It was vital that the same messages reached both internal and external groups at the right times. Akzo therefore prepared a number of communication tools, particularly for location managers briefing their employees on site:

1 An extended version of the film.
2 Slide support packs to enable management to summarize the rationale behind the identity programme.
3 A booklet summarizing the identity project.
4 A special newspaper for all 68,000 staff, published in seven languages.
5 A new international inter-company magazine in English.
6 A corporate brochure for external audiences.

The corporate message on the new identity and Akzo's new spirit was reinforced in early April by a major international advertising campaign, created jointly by PMSvW/Y&R in Holland and Collett Dickinson Pearce in London. On the marketing side, an inter-divisional marketing communication group was set up to ensure that the same message reached all possible audiences.

Implementation means making an identity visible to all audiences, and making it work practically. The Akzo identity programme will affect every communication tool produced and used by the company. That includes:

(a) Stationery – letterheads, compliment slips, etc.
(b) Corporate publications – annual report, brochures, etc.
(c) Divisional marketing communications.
(d) In-house magazines.
(e) Signs on buildings, factories.
(f) Vehicles.
(g) Uniforms.
(h) Packaging.
(i) Advertising.
(j) Forms.

Comprehensive guidelines have been produced in the form of an identity manual. This lays down the law about consistent use of the Akzo identity in terms of:

1 Corporate mark.
2 Corporate colours.
3 Corporate typeface.
4 Applications of the logo.

Further reading

No bibliography can hope to be comprehensive or to remain up-to-date for long. This brief collection of suggestions from contributors is also inevitably unbalanced, because some aspects of the subject have so far stimulated little writing of note. Several of the titles listed contain their own recommendations for further reading.

Bernstein, David. *Image and Reality*. Holt, Reinhart and Winston.
Bland, Michael. *Employee Communications*. Kogan Page.
Bowman, Pat and Ellis, Nigel. *Manual of Public Relations*. Heinemann.
Brett, Michael. *How to Read Financial Pages*. Hutchinson Business.
Confederation of British Industry. *Statement of Principles of Employee Involvement*.
Cooke, Terence E. *Mergers and Acquisitions*. Oxford UP.
Fallon, Ivan and Srodes, James. *Takeovers*.
Hayes, Roger and Watts, Reginald. *Corporate Revolution – New Strategies for Executive Leadership*. Heinemann.
House of Lords Select Committee on the European Communities (1986–7). Fourth Report, *European Broadcasting*. HMSO.
Howard, Wilfred, ed. *The Practice of Public Relations*. Heinemann.
Hutton, Peter. *Survey Research for Managers*. Macmillan.
Industrial Participation Association. *Profit-Sharing and Employee Shareholding Report*.
Industrial Society. *The Manager's Responsibility for Communications*.
Institute of Personnel Management. *Communications in Practice*.
Institute of Public Relations City and Financial Group. *Guide to the City for Professional Communicators*.
International Stock Exchange. *Admission of Securities to Listing*.
—— *The City Code on Takeovers and Mergers and the Rules Governing Substantial Acquisition of Shares*.
Jackson, Peter C. *Corporate Communication for Managers*. London: Pitman.
—— *The House Journal Handbook*. Industrial Society.

Marcus, Bruce W. *Competing for Capital in the '80s*. US: Quorum Books.

Olins, Wally. *Corporate Personality*. Design Council.

Rappaport, Alfred. *Creating Shareholder Value*. New York: Macmillan.

Regester, Michael. *Crisis Management*. Hutchinson Business.

Regulators, The: Working with the Financial Services Act, The. Faxpak Publishing.

Securities and Investments Board. *Financial Services: a Guide to the New Regulatory System*.

—— *Investors' Rights*.

—— *Self-Defence for Investors*.

Vista Survey of Employee Communications in British Industry, The. Annual. Vista Communications.

Who's Who in Financial Journalism. Dewe Rogerson.

Worcester, Robert M. and Downham, John. *The Consumer Market Research Handbook*. McGraw-Hill.

Index